Grab-and-Go!™

TEACHER GUIDE and ACTIVITY RESOURCES

Teacher Notes
- Math Centers
- Math Readers
- Practice Games

Activity Support Masters
- Math Centers Resources
- Gameboard Copymasters
- Workmats

HOUGHTON MIFFLIN HARCOURT
School Publishers

www.hmhschool.com

Contents

Teacher Notes: Math Readers

Math Centers Resources

Math Centers Resources (continued)

Math Centers Resources (continued)

Grab-and-Go!™ Kit Overview

The Grab-and-Go!™ Kit is a collection of literature, activities, and games that can be used in the math classroom. The Kit's ready-made components minimize preparation time for you and provide engaging and fun-filled ways for your students to review and reinforce valuable math skills.

Kit Components

MATH CENTERS

These ready-made, easy-to-follow activities help you reinforce or extend mathematical concepts and skills. There are three types of Math Centers – Computation and Mental Math, Geometry and Measurement, and Challenge.

LITERATURE

Integrate reading and math with these engaging stories. Through these readers, you can connect math topics and concepts to each other and to daily life.

GAMES

Practice skills and apply concepts with these ready-to-use interactive math adventures. Students can play these games in pairs or small groups.

TEACHER GUIDE AND ACTIVITY RESOURCES

This valuable resource provides everything you and your students need, including teacher notes for activities, literature, and games, and activity support masters.

Using the Grab-and-Go!™ Kit

The Grab-and-Go!™ Kit provides teachers with streamlined and enjoyable ways to help students review, reinforce, and extend math concepts and skills. The math center activities, games, and readers are designed for flexible usage – students can work independently, in pairs, small groups, or with guidance from the teacher.

- Games help students practice essential math skills in an engaging and enjoyable manner. Your students will want to play these games several times, allowing them ample hands-on practice and mastery of essential skills.

- Math Readers integrate math skills with real world situations and cross-curricular subject matter to engage student interest. Interactive questions throughout the readers focus on key concepts and support student comprehension. A responding page includes questions and an activity for additional practice after they read.

- Math Centers cover three themes: Computation and Mental Math, Geometry and Measurement, and Challenge. Colorful and creative visuals guide the student through the steps. The clear step-by-step format helps the student easily access, process, and reproduce the concepts and skills.

- Grab-and-Go!™ Teacher Guide and Activity Resources (See following page for more details.)

Using Grab-and-Go!™ Teacher Guide and Activity Resources

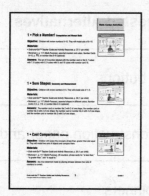

Teacher Notes for Math Centers include

- objectives for each activity
- materials needed for the activity
- answers to all the activity questions

Teacher Notes for Math Readers include

- key skills and concepts
- story summary
- essential vocabulary words
- responding answers

Teacher Notes for Games include

- objectives for each game
- materials for the game
- game instructions

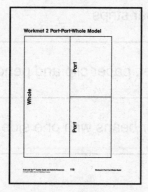

Activity Support Masters include

- Math Centers Resources
- Gameboards
- Game Resources
- Workmats

Suggested Alternatives for Math Manipulatives

Math Manipulatives	Suggested Alternatives
	seashells, pasta, buttons
	bills made from construction paper and markers
	number cards, spinners
	real coins, buttons
	paper clips, string and beads, or pasta
	buttons, coins, beans
	clock face with two lengths of string fastened to the center for hands
	cans, boxes, balls, cones, modeling clay shapes
	shapes cut out of different-colored construction paper or cardboard
	grid paper cutouts
	one-inch grid paper strips
	construction paper, paper clip and pencil
	coins, washers, or beans with one side painted

1 • Pick a Number! Computation and Mental Math

Objective: Children will review numbers 6–10. They will model sets of 6–10.

Materials:

- *Grab-and-Go!™ Teacher Guide and Activity Resources*, p. 37 (1 per child)
- Workmat 1, p. 117 (Multi-Purpose), assorted counters and cubes, Number Cards 6–10, p. 112, or number tiles 6–9 (optional)

Answers: The set of 6 counters labeled with the number card or tile 6; 7 cubes with 7; 8 cubes with 8; 9 cubes with 9; and 10 cubes with number card 10.

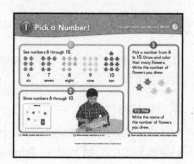

1 • Sure Shapes Geometry and Measurement

Objective: Children will review numbers 0–5. They will model sets of 1–5.

Materials:

- *Grab-and-Go!™ Teacher Guide and Activity Resources,* p. 38 (1 per child)
- Workmat 1, p. 117 (Multi-Purpose), assorted shapes in different colors, Number Cards 2–5, p. 112, or number tiles 2–5 (optional)

Answers: Sample answer: The number card or number tile 2 with 2 of one shape; the number card or number tile 3 with 3 of one shape; the number card or number tile 4 with 4 of one shape; and the number card or number tile 5 with 5 of one shape.

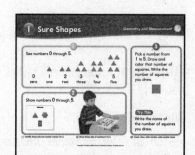

1 • Cool Comparisons Challenge

Objective: Children will review the concepts of less than, greater than and equal to. They will model two sets of objects and compare them.

Materials:

- *Grab-and-Go!™ Teacher Guide and Activity Resources,* p. 39 (1 per child)
- Workmat 1, p. 117 (Multi-Purpose), 20 counters, phrase cards for "is less than," "is greater than," and "is equal to"

Answers: Any true statement made by placing phrases between two sets of counters is correct.

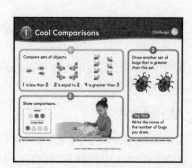

2 • Skip It Computation and Mental Math

Objective: Students will review skip counting by 2s. They will model skip counting by 2s.

Materials:

- *Grab-and-Go!™ Teacher Guide and Activity Resources*, p. 40 (1 per child)
- Workmat 1, p. 117 (Multi-Purpose), 16 pairs of cubes, Number Cards 2, 4, 6, 8, 10, 12, 14, and 16, p. 112 and p. 116

Answers: The number cards are placed in order on the workmat with a pair of cubes over each number.

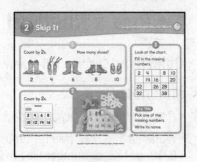

2 • Five Alive! Geometry and Measurement

Objective: Students will review skip counting by 5s. They will model skip counting by 5s.

Materials:

- *Grab-and-Go!™ Teacher Guide and Activity Resources*, p. 41 (1 per child)
- Workmat 1, p. 117 (Multi-Purpose), 40 cubes in groups of five, number cards labeled 5, 10, 15, 20, 25, 30, 35, and 40

Answers: The number cards are placed in order on the workmat with groups of five cubes over each number.

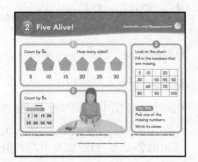

2 • Double Digit Challenge

Objective: Students will review skip counting by 10s. They will model skip counting by 10s.

Materials:

- *Grab-and-Go!™ Teacher Guide and Activity Resources*, p. 42 (1 per child)
- Workmat 1, (Multi-Purpose) p. 117, 10 tens rods, number cards labeled 10, 20, 30, 40, 50, 60, 70, 80, 90, and 100

Answers: The number cards are placed in order on the workmat with a tens rod over each number.

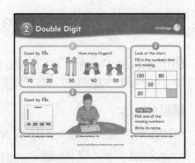

3 • Sum Sentences Computation and Mental Math

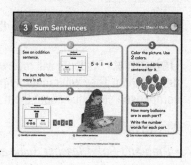

Objective: Students will review the concept of addition and parts of an addition sentence. They will model various addition sentences.

Materials:

• *Grab-and-Go!™ Teacher Guide and Activity Resources*, p. 43 (1 per child)

• Workmat 2, p. 118 (Part-Part-Whole Model), 20 counters, a double set of Number Cards, p. 112 and p. 116, or number tiles 1–9, plus and equal tiles (optional)

Answers: Any properly modeled addition sentence is correct.

3 • Put It Together Geometry and Measurement

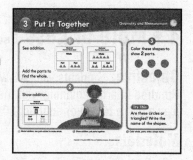

Objective: Students will review the concept of addition. They will model addition problems showing the whole and its parts.

Materials:

• *Grab-and-Go!™ Teacher Guide and Activity Resources*, p. 44 (1 per child)

• Workmat 2, p. 118 (Part-Part-Whole Model), 7 counters, Number Cards 5, 6, and 7, p. 112, or number tiles 5, 6, and 7 (optional)

Answers: A correct response is to model the numbers 5 and 6 as the sum of two parts.

3 • How Many Ways? Challenge

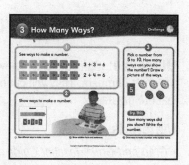

Objective: Students will review the concept of addition and parts of an addition sentence. They will model a number as the sum of two parts, exploring different addition facts.

Materials:

• *Grab-and-Go!™ Teacher Guide and Activity Resources*, p. 45 (1 per child)

• Workmat 1, p.117 (Multi-Purpose), cubes, Number Cards, p. 112 and p. 116, or number tiles 1–9, plus and equal (optional)

Answers: A correct response is showing two or more ways to achieve the same sum and labeling each with a true addition sentence.

4 • 20 Through 50 Computation and Mental Math

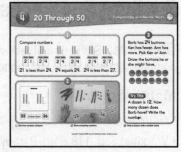

Objective: Students will review the concepts of less than, equal to, and greater than. They will randomly pick two numbers, model them, and create a comparison sentence about them.

Materials:

• *Grab-and-Go!™ Teacher Guide and Activity Resources*, p. 46 (1 per child)

• Workmat 1, p. 117 (Multi-Purpose), base-ten blocks, and 18 unit blocks, cards reading "is less than," "is equal to," and "is greater than"; and number cards labeled 22, 26, 34, 34, 37, 42, and 49

Answers: After choosing two numbers at random, the student will model each with base-ten blocks on the workmat. Then the student will form a true comparison sentence by placing a phrase between the two number cards such as, "24 is equal to 24."

4 • More or Less Geometry and Measurement

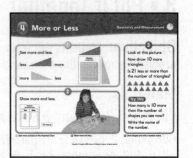

Objective: Students will review the concept of "more" and "less" using a Hundred Chart. Beginning with the number 25 modeled on the workmat, they will play a game to add or subtract 10 or 1.

Materials:

• *Grab-and-Go!™ Teacher Guide and Activity Resources*, p. 47 (1 per child)

• Workmats 3, p. 119 (Tens and Ones Chart) and 4, p. 120 (Hundred Chart), base-ten blocks, a double set of cards reading "10 more," "10 less," "1 more," and "1 less"

Answers: After randomly choosing a card, the student will either add or subtract 10 or 1 from the initial number of 25 modeled on the mat, until the blocks are gone or time runs out.

4 • Put Them in Order Challenge

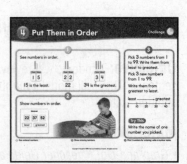

Objective: Students will review the concept of "least" and "greatest," and of ordering numbers. They will choose three numbers at random and order them from least to greatest.

Materials:

• *Grab-and-Go!™ Teacher Guide and Activity Resources*, p. 48 (1 per child)

• Workmat 1, p. 117 (Multi-Purpose), cards reading "least" and "greatest"; and number cards labeled 22, 28, 34, 37, 45, 48, 52, 57, 66, 68, 71, 77, 83, 88, 91, and 99

Answers: The words "least" and "greatest" are placed left to right on the workmat. After choosing three number cards at random, the student will correctly order the numbers left to right from least to greatest.

5 • Apples Away Computation and Mental Math

Objective: Students will review the concept of subtraction and parts of a subtraction sentence. They will model various subtraction sentences.

Materials:

• *Grab-and-Go!™ Teacher Guide and Activity Resources*, p. 49 (1 per child)

• Workmat 2, p. 118 (Part-Part-Whole Model), counters, Number Cards, p. 112 and p. 116, or number tiles 1–9, minus and equal tiles (optional)

Answers: Any correctly modeled subtraction sentence is acceptable.

5 • Runaway Squares Geometry and Measurement

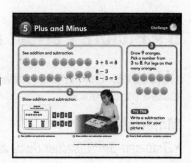

Objective: Students will review the concept of subtraction. They will model subtraction problems showing one part subtracted from the whole and the difference.

Materials:

• *Grab-and-Go!™ Teacher Guide and Activity Resources*, p. 50 (1 per child)

• Workmat 2, p. 118 (Part-Part-Whole Model), counters, Number Cards 1–5, p. 112, or number tiles 1–5 (optional)

Answers: A correct response is modeling a subtraction problem with counters and showing a number tile as the difference.

5 • Plus and Minus Challenge

Objective: Students will review the concept of addition and subtraction as inverse operations. They will model a whole and two parts and show corresponding addition and subtraction sentences.

Materials:

• *Grab-and-Go!™ Teacher Guide and Activity Resources*, p. 51 (1 per child)

• Workmat 2, p. 118 (Part-Part- Whole Model), counters, double set of Number Cards 1–9, p. 112 and p. 116, or double sets of number tiles 1–9, plus, minus, and equal tiles (optional)

Answers: A correct response is to first model a number and its two parts, then to show an addition and subtraction sentence (related facts) to reflect the model.

6 • Tally Ho! Computation and Mental Math

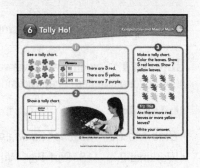

Objective: Children will review how to make and read a tally chart. They will make a tally chart.

Materials:

• *Grab-and-Go!™ Teacher Guide and Activity Resources*, p. 52 (1 per child)

• Workmat 1, p. 117 (Multi-Purpose), assorted figures, erasable marker, graph chart paper

Answers: A figure is placed or drawn in the first square of each row on the workmat. Student draws tally marks (in groups of 5) next to each figure on the workmat or on the graph chart paper. Sample answer: triangle: 6, and square: 3.

6 • Graph Math Geometry and Measurement

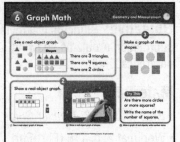

Objective: Children will review how to make and read a real-object graph. They will make a real-object graph.

Materials:

• *Grab-and-Go!™ Teacher Guide and Activity Resources*, p. 53 (1 per child)

• Workmat 1, p. 117 (Multi-Purpose), assorted figures, Number Cards 2–4, and 6, p. 112, or number tiles 2–4 and 6 (optional), two-color counters, Two- and Three Dimensional Figures, pp. 113–114, erasable marker, graph chart paper

Answers: Sample answer: the "square" has four squares and the number tile 4 placed to the right of the row.

6 • Picture Perfect Challenge

Objective: Children will review how to make and read a picture graph. They will make a picture graph.

Materials:

• *Grab-and-Go!™ Teacher Guide and Activity Resources*, p. 54 (1 per child)

• Workmat 6, p. 122 (Ten Frames), counters, classroom items, graph chart paper

Answers: One of each classroom item is placed at the left of each row of the workmat. In the frame, the number of counters matches the number of items. For example: 3 erasers, 4 pencils, 4 rubber bands, 5 paper clips, and so on.

7 • Double Trouble Computation and Mental Math

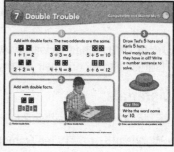

Objective: Students will review addition with double facts. They will model an addition problem using number cubes and write the addition sentence with number cards or tiles.

Materials:

- *Grab-and-Go!™ Teacher Guide and Activity Resources*, p. 55 (1 per child)
- Workmat 1, p. 117 (Multi-Purpose), two number cubes, a double set of Number Cards 1–6, p. 112, Number Cards 8, 10, 12, p. 116, or a double set of number tiles 1–6, number tiles 8, 10, 12, plus and equal signs (optional)

Answers: (a pair of 1s, 1 + 1 = 2), (a pair of 2s, 2 + 2 = 4), (a pair of 3s, 3 + 3 = 6), (a pair of 4s, 4 + 4 = 8), (a pair of 5s, 5 + 5 = 10), and (a pair of 6s, 6 + 6 = 12).

7 • Back and Forth Geometry and Measurement

Objective: Students will review the commutative property of addition. Students will match and model pairs of addition sentences.

Materials:

- *Grab-and-Go!™ Teacher Guide and Activity Resources*, p. 56 (1 per child)
- Workmat 1, p. 117 (Multi-Purpose), 10 green and 10 blue cubes, addition sentence cards labeled: 2 + 5 = 7, 5 + 2 = 7, 4 + 5 = 9, 5 + 4 = 9, 2 + 3 = 5, 3 + 2 = 5, 6 + 4 = 10, and 4 + 6 = 10

Answers: Matched pair of addition sentences and models, with addends in different positions.

7 • Another Way to Add Challenge

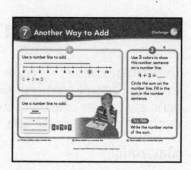

Objective: Students will review addition using a number line. They will choose two addends with a sum of 10 or less, write an addition sentence with number cards or tiles, and then move a triangle left to right on a number line to show addition.

Materials:

- *Grab-and-Go!™ Teacher Guide and Activity Resources*, p. 57 (1 per child)
- Workmat 7, p. 123 (Number Lines 1–60), a triangle, Number Cards 1–10, p. 112, or number tiles 1–10, plus and equal (optional)

Answers: Any number sentence correctly written and modeled on the number line.

8 • Spin Around Computation and Mental Math

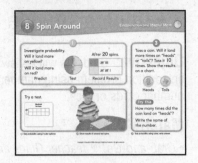

Objective: Children will review probability. They will spin a two-color spinner 10 times and record their results on a ten-frame workmat.

Materials:

- *Grab-and-Go!™ Teacher Guide and Activity Resources*, p. 58 (1 per child)
- Workmat 5, p. 121 (Ten Frame), Spinner, p. 115, two-color counters

Answers: Will vary. Results should be about 50% red and 50% yellow.

8 • Pass the Bar Geometry and Measurement

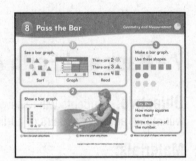

Objective: Children will review how to make and read a bar-type graph. They will make and show a graph using counters on a double ten-frame workmat.

Materials:

- *Grab-and-Go!™ Teacher Guide and Activity Resources*, p. 59 (1 per child)
- Workmat 6, p. 122 (Ten Frames), assorted counters and shapes, Number Cards 1–5, p. 112, or number tiles 1–5 (optional)

Answers: The double ten-frame workmat is shown vertically with a shape below each column and the numbers 5, 4, 3, 2, and 1 to the left of the grid. Sample answer: 4 counters in the circle column, 4 counters in the square column, and 5 counters in the triangle column.

8 • How Likely Is It? Challenge

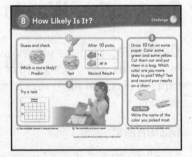

Objective: Children will review the concept of probability. They will review conducting an experiment with two unequally likely outcomes. From a bag of 7 green and 3 yellow cubes, they will randomly choose a cube from the container, record the event, return the cube, and draw again. They will repeat this ten times.

Materials:

- *Grab-and-Go!™ Teacher Guide and Activity Resources*, p. 60 (1 per child)
- Workmat 6, p. 122 (Ten Frames), cubes, counters, container

Answers: Answers will vary.

9 • Subtract! Computation and Mental Math

Objective: Students will model the concept of more and fewer, using subtraction to compare two sets of objects.

Materials:

- *Grab-and-Go!™ Teacher Guide and Activity Resources*, p. 61 (1 per child)
- Workmat 1, p. 117 (Multi-Purpose), cubes, Number Cards 1–9, p. 112, or number tiles 1–9, minus and equal tiles (optional)

Answers: Two unequal sets of cubes correctly labeled and the corresponding subtraction sentence.

9 • Picture This Geometry and Measurement

Objective: Students will model subtraction and show the corresponding subtraction sentence.

Materials:

- *Grab-and-Go!™ Teacher Guide and Activity Resources*, p. 62 (1 per child)
- Workmat 1, p. 117 (Multi-Purpose), assorted shapes in different colors, Number Cards 1–9, p. 112, or number tiles 1–9, minus and equal tiles (optional)

Answers: Choose a number to subtract from 6, circle that number of shapes and show the subtraction sentence with the correct difference.

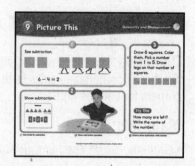

9 • Close Relatives Challenge

Objective: Students will review addition and subtraction as inverse operations and review related facts. They will show one fact family.

Materials:

- *Grab-and-Go!™ Teacher Guide and Activity Resources*, p. 63 (1 per child)
- Workmat 2, p. 118 (Part-Part-Whole Model), cubes, Number Cards 4, 5, 9, p. 112, or number tiles 4, 5, 9, and plus, minus and equal tiles (optional)

Answers: Sample answer: The following fact family shown by rearranging the tiles on the workmat: $4 + 5 = 9$, $5 + 4 = 9$, $9 - 4 = 5$, and $9 - 5 = 4$.

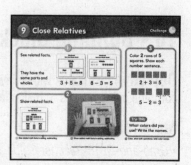

10 • More Alike Than Not Computation and Mental Math

Objective: Students will review plane figures. They sort figures by the number of sides.

Materials:

• *Grab-and-Go!™ Teacher Guide and Activity Resources*, p. 64 (1 per child)
• Workmat 1, p. 117 (Multi-Purpose), assorted figures, Number Cards 0–4, p. 112, or number tiles (optional)

Answers: Circle and oval shown with number card 0, triangles with the number tile 3, trapezoid, square, rectangle and rhombus with the number tile 4, and so on.

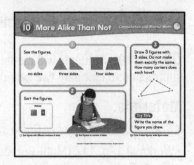

10 • On the Corner Geometry and Measurement

Objective: Students will review the attributes of plane figures, such as the number of corners and sides each one has. They will show the number of sides and corners for various figures.

Materials:

• *Grab-and-Go!™ Teacher Guide and Activity Resources*, p. 65 (1 per child)
• Workmat 1, p. 117 (Multi-Purpose), assorted figures, Number Cards 0–6, p. 112, or number tiles (optional)

Answers: The circle is shown with the number tile 0, the triangle with 3, the square, rhombus, and trapezoid with 4, and the hexagon with 6.

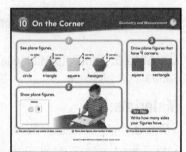

10 • Building Blocks Challenge

Objective: Students will review using plane figures as building blocks. They will combine plane figures to make new shapes.

Materials:

• *Grab-and-Go!™ Teacher Guide and Activity Resources*, p. 66 (1 per child)
• Workmat 1, p. 117 (Multi-Purpose), assorted figures

Answers: 2 trapezoids that form a hexagon; 2 squares that form a rectangle; 2 triangles that form a rhombus; 6 triangles that form a hexagon; square and 2 right triangles that form a trapezoid; and so on. Accept irregular polygons.

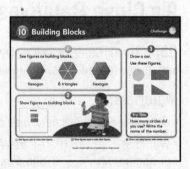

11 • Face Facts Computation and Mental Math

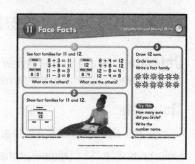

Objective: Children will review fact families. They will model fact families for 11 and 12.

Materials:
- *Grab-and-Go!™ Teacher Guide and Activity Resources*, p. 67 (1 per child)
- Workmat 2, p. 118 (Part-Part-Whole Model), Number Cards 1–9, p. 112 and p. 116, or number tiles 1–9, plus, minus, and equal tiles (optional)

Answers: Children model at least one fact family for 11 and one for 12. They place the numbers in the "whole" and "parts" section, and change the position of the plus, minus, and equal cards or tiles on the mat. They may also respond by saying or writing the fact family.

11 • Any Way You Cut It Geometry and Measurement

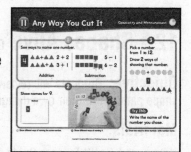

Objective: Children will review the idea that any number can be expressed as the sum of an addition sentence, or the difference of a subtraction sentence. They will model several ways to express the number 9.

Materials:
- *Grab-and-Go!™ Teacher Guide and Activity Resources*, p. 68 (1 per child)
- Workmat 1, p. 112 (Multi-Purpose), Number Cards 1–9, p. 112 and p. 116, or number tiles 1–9, minus and equal tiles (optional)

Answers: Any true addition sentence with a sum of 9. Any true subtraction sentence with a difference of 9.

11 • Problem Solving Challenge

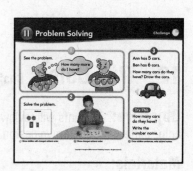

Objective: Children will review the problem-solving strategy of choosing the correct operation to solve a problem. They will use a picture to formulate the problem and gather information needed to solve it. Then they will choose an operation to get a correct answer. They may model the problem if needed.

Materials:
- *Grab-and-Go!™ Teacher Guide and Activity Resources*, p. 69 (1 per child)
- Workmat 1, p. 117 (Multi-Purpose), Number Cards 2, 3, 5, and 8, p. 112 and p. 116, or number tiles 2, 3, 5, and 8, plus, minus, and equal tiles (optional), counters

Answers: $5 - 3 = 2$ is correct. However, children may also compare groups of counters or find the missing addend ($3 + ? = 5$) to get the answer.

12 • Number Patterns Computation and Mental Math

Objective: Students will review number patterns. They will create one or more number patterns of their own design.

Materials:
- *Grab-and-Go!™ Teacher Guide and Activity Resources*, p. 70 (1 per child)
- Workmat 1, p. 117 (Multi-Purpose), 4 sets of Number Cards 1–4, p. 112 or number tiles 1, 2, 3, and 4 (optional)

Answers: Any repeating number pattern is acceptable.

12 • Shapes Alive Geometry and Measurement

Objective: Students will review shape patterns. They will create one or more shape patterns of their own design.

Materials:
- *Grab-and-Go!™ Teacher Guide and Activity Resources*, p. 71 (1 per child)
- Workmat 1, p. 117 (Multi-Purpose), shapes: circle, square, triangle

Answers: Any repeating shape pattern is acceptable.

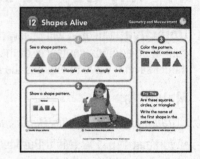

12 • True Colors Challenge

Objective: Students will review color patterns. They will create one or more color patterns of their own design.

Materials:
- *Grab-and-Go!™ Teacher Guide and Activity Resources*, p. 72 (1 per child)
- Workmat 1, p. 117 (Multi-Purpose), cubes in red, green, blue, and yellow

Answers: Any repeating color pattern is acceptable.

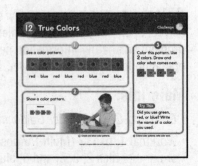

13 • Capacity Computation and Mental Math

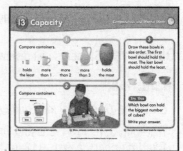

Objective: Children will review the relative capacity of containers. They will compare containers to judge which holds more and which holds less.

Materials:

• *Grab-and-Go!™ Teacher Guide and Activity Resources*, p. 73 (1 per child)

• Workmat 1, p. 117 (Multi-Purpose), assorted classroom containers, cards reading "less" and "more"

Answers: Children choose two containers at random and determine by observation only which would hold more and which would hold less.

13 • Heavy and Light Geometry and Measurement

Objective: Children will review the concept of weight and the relative weight of objects. They will compare two classroom objects to determine which is heavier and which is lighter.

Materials:

• *Grab-and-Go!™ Teacher Guide and Activity Resources*, p. 74 (1 per child)

• Workmat 1, p. 117 (Multi-Purpose), assorted objects, cards reading "heavier" and "lighter"

Answers: Children choose two items at random and lift to see which one is heavier. They correctly label them "heavier" or "lighter" and repeat with other pairs of items.

13 • Hot and Cold Challenge

Objective: Children will review the concept of temperature and the relative temperature of things such as familiar food items. They will use past experience to determine the relative temperature of items in pictures.

Materials:

• *Grab-and-Go!™ Teacher Guide and Activity Resources*, p. 75 (1 per child)

• Workmat 1, p. 117 (Multi-Purpose), pictures of familiar hot and cold food items from magazines, cards reading "hot" and "cold"

Answers: Children choose two items at random. From past experience and picture clues, they determine which item is hot and which is cold and correctly label each "hot" or "cold." They repeat the task with other pairs of items.

14 • Teen Time Computation and Mental Math

Objective: Students will review place value. They will model numbers 11 to 19.

Materials:

• *Grab-and-Go!™ Teacher Guide and Activity Resources*, p. 76 (1 per child)

• Workmat 3, p. 119 (Tens and Ones Chart), 19 cubes, Number Cards, two number 1 and numbers 2–9, p. 112, or two number 1 tiles and tiles 2–9 (optional)

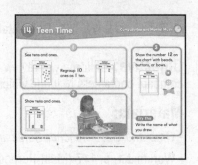

Answers: Correctly modeled numbers 11–19. A train of ten cubes in the tens section and the number tile 1 shown beneath it and single cubes from 1 to 9 in the ones section and the corresponding number tile beneath them.

14 • Groups of Ten Geometry and Measurement

Objective: Students will review groups of ten. They will model numbers 10, 20, 30, 40, and 50.

Materials:

• *Grab-and-Go!™ Teacher Guide and Activity Resources*, p. 76 (1 per child)

• Workmat 5, p. 121 (Ten Frame), 50 cubes, number cards labeled 10, 20, 30, 40, and 50

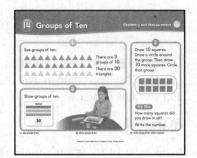

Answers: The number 10 is shown with one train of 10 cubes, 20 with two ten-trains, 30 with three ten-trains, 40 with four ten-trains, and 50 with five ten-trains.

14 • Ten and Up Challenge

Objective: Students will review place value and numbers from 10 to 50. They will model numbers 17, 24, 29, 36, 42 and 49.

Materials:

• *Grab-and-Go!™ Teacher Guide and Activity Resources*, p. 78 (1 per child)

• Workmat 3, p. 119 (Tens and Ones Chart), 50 cubes, Number Cards 1–9, p. 112 or number tiles 1–9 (optional), number cards labeled 17, 24, 29, 36, 42, and 49

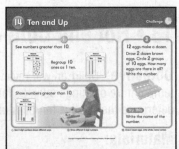

Answers: The number card 17 is shown under the workmat with 1 train of 10 cubes and number card or tile 1 in the tens place; and 7 cubes and number card or tile 7 in the ones place. 24 is shown as 2 ten-trains and number card or tile 2 in the tens place; and 4 cubes and number card or tile 4 in the ones place. Other numbers are modeled in the same manner.

15 • A Nickel is Five Computation and Mental Math

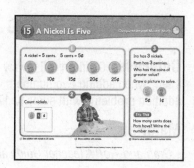

Objective: Students will review the value of a nickel and skip-counting by 5s. They will show sets of nickels and their value.

Materials:

• *Grab-and-Go!™ Teacher Guide and Activity Resources*, p. 79 (1 per child)

• Workmat 1, p. 117 (Multi-Purpose), 10 nickels, number cards labeled 5, 10, 15, 20, 25, 30, 35, 40, 45, 50, and a card labeled with the ¢ sign

Answers: A random set of nickels is placed on the mat. Students skip-counting to find their value and show the value. They repeat this exercise several times.

15 • A Pretty Penny Geometry and Measurement

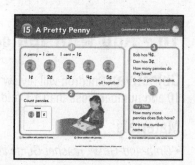

Objective: Students will review the value of a penny. They will show sets of pennies and their value.

Materials:

• *Grab-and-Go!™ Teacher Guide and Activity Resources*, p. 80 (1 per child)

• Workmat 1, p. 117 (Multi-Purpose), Number Cards 1–9, p. 112, or number tiles 1–9 (optional), 10 pennies, number card 10, and a card labeled with the ¢ sign

Answers: A random set of pennies is placed on the mat. Students count to find their value, and show the value. They repeat this exercise several times.

15 • Dime Store Challenge

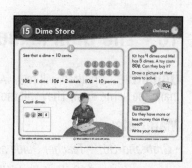

Objective: Students will review the value of pennies, nickels, and dimes and review skip-counting by 10s. They will show sets of dimes and their value.

Materials:

• *Grab-and-Go!™ Teacher Guide and Activity Resources*, p. 81 (1 per child)

• Workmat 1, p. 117 (Multi-Purpose), 10 dimes, number cards labeled 10, 20, 30, 40, 50, 60, 70, 80, 90, and 100, a card labeled with the ¢ sign

Answers: A random set of dimes is placed on the mat. Students skip-counting to find their value, and show the value. They repeat this exercise several times.

16 • Make a Ten to Add Computation and Mental Math

Objective: Children will review the problem-solving strategy of "making a ten" when adding two numbers with a sum greater than ten. They will model addition problems with sums to 17.

Materials:

- *Grab-and-Go!™ Teacher Guide and Activity Resources*, p. 82 (1 per child)
- Workmat 6, p. 122 (Ten Frames), two-color counters, Number Cards 3–9, p. 112 and p. 116, or number tiles 3–9, plus and equal tiles (optional)

Answers: Children fill up the top frame first to "make" a ten and leave the rest of the counters on the second frame. Children then write an addition sentence.

16 • Add with Ten Geometry and Measurement

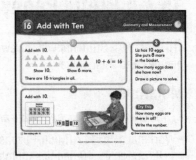

Objective: Children will review adding with 10. They will model the addition of 10 and numbers less than 10, and show corresponding addition sentences.

Materials:

- *Grab-and-Go!™ Teacher Guide and Activity Resources*, p. 83 (1 per child)
- Workmat 6, p. 122 (Ten Frames), two-color counters, Number Cards 2–9, p. 112 and p. 116, or number tiles 2–9, plus and equal tiles (optional)

Answers: Children place 10 red counters in the first frame. They pick an addend at random and show the second addend in yellow on the second frame.

16 • The Sum Is the Same Challenge

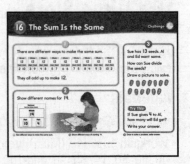

Objective: Children will review addition facts to see that there are many ways to make the same sum. They will model 14 as a whole that is a sum of two parts.

Materials:

- *Grab-and-Go!™ Teacher Guide and Activity Resources*, p. 84 (1 per child)
- Workmat 2, p. 118 (Part-Part-Whole Model), Number Cards 4–7, p. 112 and p. 116, or number tiles 4–7 (optional)

Answers: Children place 14 in the "whole" section and these addend pairs in the "parts" section, shown one pair at a time: (4,10), (5, 9), (6, 8), (7,7), (8, 6), (9, 5), and (10, 4).

17 • Half Past Computation and Mental Math

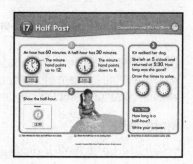

Objective: Students will review time to the hour and half hour. They will model time on an analog clock based on digital time cards.

Materials:

• *Grab-and-Go!™ Teacher Guide and Activity Resources*, p. 85 (1 per child)

• Analog Clock Model, p. 105, or demonstration clock, time cards labeled 2:30, 4:30, 6:30, 8:30, 10:30, and 12:30 in digital format

Answers: Any of the times shown on a time card chosen at random is modeled by the student on the analog clock model or demonstration clock.

17 • On the Hour Geometry and Measurement

Objective: Students will review telling time to the hour on a digital and analog clock. They will model time on an analog clock based on digital time cards.

Materials:

• *Grab-and-Go!™ Teacher Guide and Activity Resources*, p. 86 (1 per child)

• Analog Clock Model, p. 105, or demonstration clock, time cards labeled 2:00, 4:00, 6:00, 8:00, 10:00, and 12:00 in digital format

Answers: Any of the times shown on a time card chosen at random is modeled by the student on the analog clock model or demonstration clock.

17 • Time Passes Challenge

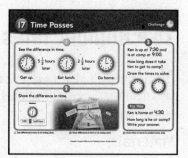

Objective: Students will review the passage of time. They will show the passage of time by adding or subtracting an hour or half hour from an analog clock based on digital time cards.

Materials:

• *Grab-and-Go!™ Teacher Guide and Activity Resources*, p. 87 (1 per child)

• Number Cards, p. 112, or number tiles, plus and minus tiles (optional), Analog Model Clock, p. 105, or, demonstration clock, time cards labeled 1:00, 3:00, 5:00, 7:00, 9:00, and 11:00 in digital format, and cards reading "half hour" and "hour"

Answers: Time shown on a randomly chosen time card is modeled on the analog clock model or demonstration clock. Students choose a plus or minus tile and "half hour" or "hour." They then move the hands on the clock forward or back to show the new time.

18 • Interchange Computation and Mental Math

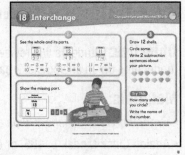

Objective: Students will review subtraction, informally explore fact families, and review the concept of addition and subtraction as inverse operations. They will model subtraction problems by showing them as a whole and its parts.

Materials:

- *Grab-and-Go!™ Teacher Guide and Activity Resources*, p. 88 (1 per child)
- Workmat 2, p. 118 (Part-Part-Whole Model), Number Cards 1–9, p. 112 and Number Cards 10–12, p. 116, or number tiles 1–9 (optional), cards labeled 9 – 4, 10 – 6, 11 – 5, and 12 – 9

Answers: Check children's work.

18 • The Missing Piece Geometry and Measurement

Objective: Students will review how to find a missing addend in a subtraction sentence. They will model subtraction facts by choosing one whole at random, modeling it, and then finding the part to subtract needed to give a difference of 4.

Materials:

- *Grab-and-Go!™ Teacher Guide and Activity Resources*, p. 89 (1 per child)
- Workmat 1, p. 117 (Multi-Purpose), Number Cards 1–9, p. 112 and p. 116, number tiles 1–9, plus and equal tiles (optional), cubes

Answers: Students choose a number at random and place that many cubes on the mat. They find and show the part to subtract needed to give a difference of 4, and remove that number of cubes from the mat. Then they complete the subtraction sentence.

18 • Number Tales Challenge

Objective: Students will review the strategy of using a picture to tell a story with numbers. They will explore fact families and model a fact family with the numbers 12, 4, and 8.

Materials:

- *Grab-and-Go!™ Teacher Guide and Activity Resources*, p. 90 (1 per child)
- Workmat 2, p. 118 (Part-Part-Whole Model), 24 cubes, Number Cards 4 and 8, p. 112, Number Card 12, p. 116, or number tiles 4 and 8; plus, minus, and equal tiles (optional)

Answers: Students place 12 cubes in the "whole" section, 4 in one part section and 8 in the other. They show the following fact family: $4 + 8 = 12$, $8 + 4 = 12$, $12 – 4 = 8$, and $12 – 8 = 4$.

19 • Parting Company Computation and Mental Math

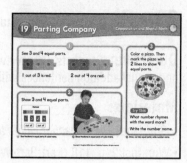

Objective: Children will review the concept of parts of a whole. They will make a train of three or four cubes that are two different colors. They will show the part of the whole each color represents.

Materials:

- *Grab-and-Go!™ Teacher Guide and Activity Resources*, p. 91 (1 per child)
- Workmat 1, p. 117 (Multi-Purpose), cubes, Number Cards 1–4, p. 112, or number tiles 1–4 (optional), phrase card labeled "out of"

Answers: Possible answers are: 1 out of 3, 2 out of 3, 1 out of 4, 2 out of 4, and 3 out of 4.

19 • Half Math Geometry and Measurement

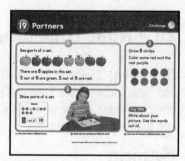

Objective: Children will review the concept of equal parts of a two-dimensional figure. They will divide a two-dimensional figure into two equal parts.

Materials:

- *Grab-and-Go!™ Teacher Guide and Activity Resources*, p. 92 (1 per child)
- Workmat 1, p. 117 (Multi-Purpose), assorted two-dimensional shapes, paper cutouts of circles, rectangles, rhombuses, and other shapes as needed, markers, straight objects such as a drinking straw or piece of yarn or string

Answers: Folding each figure correctly divides each shape in half.

19 • Partners Challenge

Objective: Children will review the concept of parts of a set. They will make a set of 10 two-color counters, all with the red sides up. They will spin to see how many counters they must turn over. Then they will show what part of the set the yellow counters are.

Materials:

- *Grab-and-Go!™ Teacher Guide and Activity Resources*, p. 93 (1 per child)
- Workmat 1, p. 117 (Multi-Purpose), two-color counters, Spinner, p. 115, Number Cards, p. 112, or number tiles 1–9 (optional), phrase card labeled "out of"

Answers: Possible answers are: 1 out of 10, 2 out of 10, 3 out of 10, 4 out of 10, 5 out of 10, 6 out of 10, 7 out of 10, 8 out of 10, 9 out of 10, and 10 out of 10.

20 • Regroup Computation and Mental Math

Objective: Students will review addition of two-digit numbers with regrouping and model addition sentences with two-color counters on a workmat.

Materials:

- *Grab-and-Go!™ Teacher Guide and Activity Resources*, p. 91 (1 per child)
- Workmat 2, p. 118 (Part-Part-Whole Model), 30 two-color counters, Number Cards, p. 112 and p. 116, or number tiles, including a double set of 2 tiles, number cards labeled 21–26, addition sentence cards labeled 13 + 8 =, 14 + 7 =, 15 + 9 =, 16 + 6 =, 17 + 8 =, 18 + 8 =, 18 + 4 =

Answers: Check children's work.

20 • Count On Geometry and Measurement

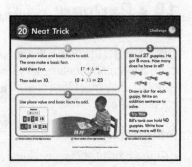

Objective: Students review the addition of two-digit numbers and counting on to add. They pick an addition card and model the problem with counters. They place one addend on a mat with red counters and as they place the second addend using yellow counters, they will count on to add.

Materials:

- *Grab-and-Go!™ Teacher Guide and Activity Resources*, p. 95 (1 per child)
- Workmat 2, p. 118 (Part-Part-Whole Model), 20 two-color counters, Number Cards, p. 112 and p. 116, or number tiles, addition cards labeled 10 + 9 =, 11 + 5 =, 12 + 3 =, 13 + 4 =, 15 + 3 =, 12 + 7 =, 16 + 1 =

Answers: Check children's work.

20 • Neat Trick Challenge

Objective: Students will review addition of two-digit numbers, using place value and basic facts to add. They will choose an addition sentence card and write two other addition sentences to solve the problem. They first add the ones. Then they add that sum to the tens.

Materials:

- *Grab-and-Go!™ Teacher Guide and Activity Resources*, p. 96 (1 per child)
- Workmat 1, p. 117 (Multi-Purpose), 2 sets of Number Cards, p. 112 and p. 116, or 2 sets of number tiles, 2 plus and 2 equal signs, number cards labeled 24, 25, and 32, addition cards labeled 18 + 7 =, 15 + 9 =, 24 + 8 =

Answers: Check children's work.

1 • Rainy Day Fun

Objective: To practice comparing numbers

Materials: *For partners* 2 playing pieces, 3-Section Spinner, p. 97, labeled 1-3, pencil, paper clip

Playing the Game: This activity gives children an opportunity to practice comparing numbers in the teens.

Partners take turns. Both partners place a game piece on START. The first player spins the pointer and moves the game piece that many spaces. If the number he or she lands on is greater than 14, the player moves his or her piece ahead one space. If the number is less than 15, the player moves the piece back one space. The first player to get to END wins the game.

2 • On the Water

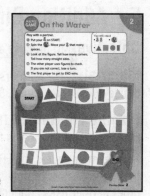

Objective: To practice describing the attributes of plane figures

Materials: *For partners* 2 playing pieces, 3-Section Spinner, p. 97, labeled 1-3, pencil, paper clip, plane figures

Playing the Game: This activity gives children an opportunity to practice describing the attributes of different plane figures.

Partners take turns. Players put their playing pieces on START. The first player spins the pointer and moves that number of spaces. Then that player looks at the figure in that space and tells the number of corners and the number of straight sides. The other player uses the plane figures to check the answer. If the answer is incorrect, that player loses a turn. The first player to get to END wins the game.

3 • The Greater Game

Objective: To practice comparing numbers

Materials: *For partners* 2 playing pieces, 3-Section Spinner, p. 97, labeled 1-3, pencil, paper clip, 20 blue connecting cubes, 20 red connecting cubes

Playing the Game: This activity gives children an opportunity to practice comparing numbers.

Partners place their playing pieces at START. Partners take turns spinning the pointer and moving a playing piece that many spaces. The player tells which of the two numbers is greater. The partner uses connecting cubes to check the answer. If the answer is incorrect, the player loses a turn. The first player to get to END wins the game.

4 • Tile Pattern Pickup

Objective: To practice making a color pattern

Materials: *For partners* 2 playing pieces, 3-Section Spinner, p. 97, labeled 1-3, pencil, paper clip, 15 red tiles, 15 blue tiles, 15 yellow tiles

Playing the Game: This activity gives children an opportunity to practice making their own color patterns.

Partners take turns. Both players put their playing pieces on START. The first player spins the pointer and moves that number of spaces. That player looks at the space and takes that number and color of tiles. When both players reach END, they use their tiles to make a pattern, using as many tiles as possible. The player who uses the most tiles in his or her pattern with no mistakes is the winner.

5 • Addition Bingo

Objective: To practice addition facts to 8

Materials: *For partners* 24 Horizontal Addition Fact Cards to 8, p. 100, 18 red counters, 8 blue connecting cubes, 8 red connecting cubes

Playing the Game: This activity gives children an opportunity to practice one-digit addition and review basic facts to 8.

Each partner covers the FREE SPACE square on his or her board with a counter. Partners then take turns randomly selecting a card and saying the sum of that fact aloud. The other partner uses connecting cubes to model and verify the sum. If the sum is correct and the first player has that number on his or her board, the player covers the number with a counter. The first player to cover three spaces in a row (horizontally, vertically, or diagonally) wins the game.

6 • Puddle Hopping

Objective: To practice naming numbers ten more and ten less

Materials: *For partners* 2 playing pieces, 4-Section Spinner, p. 97, labeled 1–4, pencil, paper clip, base-ten blocks

Playing the Game: This activity gives children an opportunity to practice naming numbers ten more and ten less than a 2-digit number.

Partners take turns. One partner spins the pointer and moves his or her playing piece that number of spaces. The player reads the number landed on and tells the number ten more and the number ten less than that number. The other player checks the answers using the base-ten blocks. If the answer is incorrect, the player loses a turn. The first player to get to END wins.

7 • Subtraction Slide

Objective: To practice subtraction facts to 8

Materials: *For partners* number cube labeled 1–6, 5 red counters, 5 yellow counters

Playing the Game: This activity gives children an opportunity to practice one-digit subtraction and review basic facts to 8.

Partners take turns. One partner tosses the number cube and subtracts that number from 8. If the difference is shown on that player's slide, he or she covers it with a counter. If the difference is not shown on the slide, the player does nothing. The first player to cover the whole slide is the winner.

8 • 10 Ahead

Objective: To practice recognizing numerical patterns.

Materials: *For partners* 2 playing pieces, 6-Section Spinner, p. 102, labeled 1-6, pencil, paper clip

Playing the Game: This activity gives children an opportunity to practice discovering numerical patterns by tens.

Partners take turns. Each partner starts by placing his or her playing piece on START. One player spins the pointer and moves that number of spaces on the hundred chart. If the player lands on green, he or she moves ahead ten spaces. If the player lands on pink, he or she moves back ten spaces. The first player who gets to END wins the game.

9 • Ducky Sums

Objective: To practice one-digit addition.

Materials: *For partners* number cube labeled 1–6, 2 playing pieces, pencil, paper clip

Playing the Game: This activity gives children an opportunity to practice one-digit addition and review basic facts to 12.

Partners take turns. The first partner rolls the number cube and moves the playing piece that many spaces. Then the partner spins the pointer and adds the number he or she spins and the number the game piece lands on to find the sum. The other partner checks the addition using paper and pencil. The first partner to get to END wins the game.

10 • Positional Bingo

Objective: To practice following positional directions

Materials: *For partners* 3-Section Spinner, p. 97, labeled "blue," "yellow," and "red"; 4-Section Spinner, p. 97, labeled "up," "down," "left," and "right"; 2 pencils; 2 paper clips; 9 red counters; 9 yellow counters

Playing the Game: This activity gives children an opportunity to practice following directional instructions.

One player uses a red counter and the other player uses a yellow counter. Partners take turns. The first player spins the pointer on the color spinner and selects a square of that color on his or her playing board and places a counter there. That same player then spins the pointer on the direction spinner and moves his or her counter one space in that direction. If the player cannot move in the indicated direction, his or her turn is over and he or she removes the counter from the board. The first player to get three counters in a row wins the game.

11 • Under the Sea

Objective: To practice subtraction facts to 12

Materials: *For partners* 1 red playing piece, 1 blue playing piece, 3-Section Spinner, p. 97, labeled 1–3, pencil, paper clip, 12 connecting cubes

Playing the Game: This activity gives children an opportunity to practice subtraction and review basic facts to 12.

Partners take turns. Both players begin at START. One partner spins the pointer and moves that many spaces. The child spins again and subtracts that number from the number the game piece is on. He or she checks the answer using connecting cubes. If the answer is not correct, or if it is not possible to subtract, then the child loses a turn. The first player to get to END wins the game.

12 • Story Time

Objective: To practice showing analog and digital times

Materials: *For partners* 2 playing pieces, 3-Section Spinner, p. 97, labeled 1-3, pencil, paper clip, Analog Clock Model, p. 105, Digital Clock Model, p. 106

Playing the Game: This activity gives children an opportunity to practice showing the same time on both analog and digital clocks.

Partners take turns. Players put their game pieces on START. The first player spins the pointer and moves that number of spaces. That player reads the clock in the space and then shows the same time on the other kind of clock. (If the board shows an analog clock, the player shows time on the digital clock, and vice versa.) If the answer is incorrect, the player loses a turn. The first player to get to END wins the game.

13 • Related Fact Race

Objective: Practice finding related subtraction facts

Materials: *For partners* 16 Horizontal Subtraction Fact Cards to 8, p. 108, 18 counters

Playing the Game: This activity gives children an opportunity to practice naming related subtraction facts to 8.

Partners take turns. The first partner picks a card at random and says the difference and the related subtraction fact. The partner checks the answer with paper and pencil. If it is correct, that player covers one space on his or her board with a counter. The first player to cover his or her entire game board wins the game.

14 • Bank It

Objective: To practice counting money

Materials: *For partners* 2 playing pieces, 4-Section Spinner, p. 97, labeled 1-4, pencil, paper clip, 12 quarters, 12 dimes, 12 nickels, 12 pennies

Playing the Game: This activity gives children an opportunity to practice making different amounts of money.

Players are each given four of each coin. The other coins are put aside for use as a bank. Players take turns. Both players put their playing pieces on START. The first player spins the pointer and moves that number of spaces. The player follows directions or uses coins to show the amount indicated on the space. The other player checks the amount. If the answer is incorrect, the player loses a turn. The first player to reach END wins the game.

15 • Graph Game

Objective: To practice making and reading a graph

Materials: *For partners* 3-Section Spinner, p. 97, labeled "red," "yellow," and "green", pencil, paper clip, 16 green tiles, 16 red tiles, 16 yellow tiles

Playing the Game: This activity gives children an opportunity to practice making and reading a bar graph.

Partners take turns. Each player spins the pointer and places a tile of the matching color on his or her graph. After both players have had six spins, the partners count the tiles for each color on the graph. The player who went last spins one more time to determine the final color. The player with the most counters for that color wins. If both players have the same number for that color, spin again.

16 • Neighborhood Sums

Objective: To practice adding numbers with sums to 20

Materials: *For partners* 2 playing pieces, 3-Section Spinner, p. 97, labeled 1-3, pencil, paper clip, Workmat 7, p. 123 (Number Lines 1-60), 9 red connecting cubes, 9 yellow connecting cubes, 9 blue connecting cubes

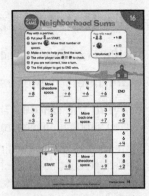

Playing the Game: This activity gives children an opportunity to practice and review sums to 20.

Partners take turns. Both players put their playing pieces on START. The first player spins the pointer and moves that number of spaces. That player finds the sum of the problem on that space. The other player uses connecting cubes to check the sum. If the sum is incorrect, the first player loses a turn. The first player to get to END wins the game.

17 • Tens and Ones Race

Objective: To practice separating numbers into tens and ones

Materials: *For partners* 2 playing pieces, 6-Section Spinner, p. 102, labeled 1-6, pencil, paper clip, base ten blocks

Playing the Game: This activity gives children an opportunity to practice decomposing numbers into tens and ones.

Partners take turns. One partner spins the pointer and moves his or her playing piece that number of spaces. That player reads the number he or she lands on and tells how many tens and how many ones. The partner checks the answer by using base ten blocks. If the answer is incorrect, the player loses a turn. The first player to get to END wins the game.

18 • Basic Facts Race

Objective: To practice finding missing numbers in addition and subtraction sentences

Materials: *For partners* 2 playing pieces, 3-Section Spinner, p. 97, labeled 1-3, pencil, paper clip, 20 connecting cubes

Playing the Game: This activity gives children an opportunity to use their knowledge of fact families to solve missing number sentences.

Partners take turns. Both players put their playing pieces on START. The first player spins the pointer and moves that number of spaces on the board. That player finds the missing number in the sentence on that space. The other player checks the answer by using connecting cubes. If the answer is incorrect, the player loses a turn. The first player who gets to END wins the game.

19 • Flying Along

Objective: To practice 2-digit addition

Materials: *For partners* 2 playing pieces, 3-Section Spinner, p. 97, labeled 1-3, pencil, paper clip, Workmat 2, p. 118 (Part-Part-Whole Model), 50 connecting cubes

Playing the Game: This activity gives children an opportunity to practice 2-digit addition with regrouping.

Partners take turns spinning the pointer and moving his or her playing piece that many spaces. That partner then writes the problem shown on the space on paper and solves it, using the workmat and connecting cubes if necessary.

Partners can check each other's work. If the sum is incorrect, the player loses a turn. The first partner to get to END wins the game.

20 • Measure Up!

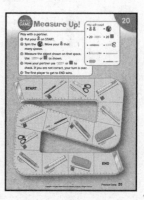

Objective: To practice measuring classroom items

Materials: *For partners* 2 playing pieces, 3-Section Spinner, p. 97, labeled 1-3, pencil, paper clip, 20 small paper clips, 20 color tiles, paintbrush, pencil, scissors, eraser, marker, crayon

Playing the Game: This activity gives children an opportunity to practice measuring classroom items with non-standard units.

Partners take turns. Both players put their playing piece on START. The first player spins the pointer and moves the playing piece that number of spaces. The player then uses paper clips to measure the actual object shown in that square of the board. The other player also measures to check. If the answer is incorrect, the player loses a turn. The first player to get to END wins the game.

April's First Word
by Suzanne Shaffer illustrated by Cathy Johnson

Focus: solid figures

Story Summary: In *April's First Word*, a mother and son try to get baby April to talk. They point to different holes on a toy board, asking April which figure goes in each hole. Finally, April comes up with the figure that has the most difficult name, and April says, "cylinder"!

Vocabulary: shape, face, cube, sphere, cone, cylinder

Responding Answers:
Draw Children find pages 4 and 5 and draw a cube and a cone.
Tell About Children tell about a cube and a cone.
Write Children write: *sphere and pyramid.*

Astronaut Arrangement
by Paco Hernandez illustrated by Jane McCreary

Focus: fractions

Story Summary: In *Astronaut Arrangement*, four children play with 24 action toys and try to find a way to share the toys in equal parts.

Vocabulary: equal parts, share

Responding Answers:
Draw Children find page 3 and draw one stick figure for Roger and put 14 Xs next to it. They should draw another stick figure for Will and put 10 Xs next to that figure.
Tell About Children tell that there are 24 (twenty-four) astronauts in all. Roger and Will do not have equal shares.
Write Children write: *12 astronauts.*

Busy Bugs
by Sarah Hughes illustrated by Bob Barner

Focus: addition facts through 10

Story Summary: In *Busy Bugs,* a narrator talks about the number of ants, flowers, and butterflies there are in the different illustrations. In each illustration, there are sets of bugs, and readers are asked to add and find the total.

Vocabulary: how many, how many more

Responding Answers:
Draw Children find page 7 and draw 10 butterflies.
Tell About Children tell that the butterflies are alike because they are all blue. Children tell that there are 6 butterflies resting and 4 flying.
Write Children write: *10 butterflies in all.*

Ducks In a Pond
by Linda Carroll illustrated by Eileen Hine

Focus: numbers 10 through 20

Story Summary: In *Ducks in a Pond*, 10 ducks are on their way to swim in a pond. They pick up 1 duck, and when they arrive at the pond, 6 ducks are already swimming in the pond. Two more join, making 20 ducks. At the end, they all fly away.

Vocabulary: how many, numbers 10 through 20

Responding Answers:
Draw Children find page 5 and make 17 Xs to show each duck in the pond.
Tell About Children tell that there are 10 ducks on the left and 7 ducks on the right. There are 17 ducks in all.
Write Children write: *17 or There are 17 ducks in all.*

Funny Bunny Hats
by Ramon Perez illustrated by Jannie Ho

Focus: addition strategies

Story Summary: In *Funny Bunny Hats,* a bunny makes funny hats. She makes them for the different animals that come to her shop. Page by page, readers add the hats Bunny makes.

Vocabulary: how many, add

Responding Answers:
Draw Children find page 6 and draw Cat's 6 hats and Bunny's 10 hats.
Tell About Children tell that Cat has 6 hats and she wants 10 more. Cat will have 16 hats.
Write Children write: *16 hats in all.*

Garden Party
by Pepe Ramirez illustrated by John Berg

Focus: subtracting from two-digit numbers

Story Summary: In *Garden Party*, two caterpillars decide to have a party in Mr. Green's garden. Other caterpillars come, and they eat from the garden. Readers subtract the number of different vegetables eaten from the original number of vegetables in the garden.

Vocabulary: subtract, how many left, digit

Responding Answers:
Draw Children find page 3 and draw the garden with 7 heads of lettuce and 9 Xs.
Tell About Children tell that Mr. Green planted 16 heads of lettuce, and the caterpillars ate 9 of them.
Write Children write: *7 heads are left.*

It's a Homerun!
by Julio Lopez illustrated by Molly Delaney

Focus: adding 2-digit and 1-digit numbers

Story Summary: In *It's a Homerun!,* Maria collects different sets of baseball cards. Her brother gives her several cards for one pack, Maria buys cards from Mrs. Santos to complete another set, she shows her friend Carrie cards she has, and at the end, her mother finds the cards to complete the last set.

Vocabulary: add, how many, digit

Responding Answers:
Draw Children find page 2 and draw 7 cards.
Tell About Children tell that there are 7 cards.
Write Children write: *Maria has 56 cards.*

Join Us
by Lita Davis illustrated by Noah Jones

Focus: addition concepts

Story Summary: In *Join Us*, two girls have a large rubber ball. In ones, twos, and threes, other children join them until they have the 10 children they need to form a circle and throw each other the ball.

Vocabulary: how many, add

Responding Answers:
Draw Children find page 3 and draw 5 stick figures.
Tell About Children tell that there are 3 children on the playground and 2 are joining them.
Write Children write: *5 children in all.*

Ken's Coins
by Carole Forsberg illustrated by Rusty Fletcher

Focus: the value of coins

Story Summary: In *Ken's Coins*, Ken's dad hides different coins under objects in the kitchen. The objects are clues that Ken uses to find the coins. For example, he finds a nickel under a bowl of five apples.

Vocabulary: penny, nickel, dime, quarter

Responding Answers:
Draw Children find page 5 and draw 10 cans of soup.
Tell About Children tell that there are 10 cans of soup and Ken will find a dime under one of them.
Write Children write: *There is a dime.*

Milk for Sale
by Camille Torez illustrated by Diana Schoenbrun

Focus: subtraction facts through 10

Story Summary: In *Milk for Sale,* Cora the Cow hopes to sell her 10 bottles of milk. Different animals come along and Cora likes them enough to give them bottles of milk. At the end, only one bottle is left, and she shares it with a kitten.

Vocabulary: count back, more, fewer

Responding Answers:
Draw Children find page 4 and draw 8 bottles on a table.
Tell About Children tell that these are 6 bottles on the table and Cora gave Dana Deer 2 bottles.
Write Children write: *6 bottles left.*

Miss Bumble's Garden
by Juan Delgado illustrated by Sally Vitsky

Focus: subtraction strategies

Story Summary: In *Miss Bumble's Garden,* chipmunks, crows, rabbits, foxes, and a hen come to steal vegetables from Miss Bumble's garden. Page by page, readers subtract what the animals take from the whole garden.

Vocabulary: how many left, count back

Responding Answers:
Draw Children find page 4 and draw 6 crows and 6 heads of lettuce.
Tell About Children tell that Miss Bumble planted 15 heads of lettuce and the crows have 6 heads of lettuce.
Write Children write: *Mrs. Bumble has 9 heads of lettuce left.*

Name That Number
by Carlo Perez illustrated by Jamie Smith

Focus: comparing and ordering numbers

Story Summary: In *Name That Number,* two teams compete to name the numbers that will complete a large hundred chart. Children answer questions in the text, such as, "What number comes between 50 and 52?" The score is tied at the end of the story.

Vocabulary: pattern, hundred chart, before, between

Responding Answers:
Draw Children find page 7 and draw the numbers 12 and 17.
Tell About Children tell that the numbers 33, 35, 36, and 38 are missing.
Write Children write: *one hundred.*

Picture Puzzles
by Melvin Jefferson illustrated by Julia Gorton

Focus: addition and subtraction facts through 12

Story Summary: In *Picture Puzzles*, a sister and brother play with geometric shapes to make picture puzzles. The girl makes a boat with a sail out of four triangles. The two siblings make other shapes and at the end use them to build a rocket ship.

Vocabulary: shape, triangle, square

Responding Answers:
Draw Children find page 7 and draw the rocket ship.
Tell About Children tell that the rocket ship is made with 4 triangles and 6 squares.
Write Children write: *10 pieces.*

Rolling Snowballs
by Michael Delgado illustrated by Mircea Catusanu

Focus: weight

Story Summary: In *Rolling Snowballs*, three polar bears roll snowballs up the hill to make a snow bear. One polar bear easily rolls the smallest ball. Two bears roll the middle-size ball. It takes all three polar bears to roll the large snowball up the hill, where they make their snow bear.

Vocabulary: heavy, heavier, heaviest

Responding Answers:
Draw Children find pages 4 and 5 and draw 3 different-sized snowballs: smallest, in between, and largest.
Tell About Children tell that 3 bears are needed because the largest ball is too heavy for one or two bears.
Write Children write: *The 3 bears are pushing the largest snowball.*

Drew's Shoes
by Jackie Mallory illustrated by Liz Callen

Focus: number patterns

Story Summary: In *Drew's Shoes*, a young boy decides to give away shoes that he no longer wears. To count the shoes, he counts by twos. One shoe is missing when they are all counted, but the cat comes walking in with it.

Vocabulary: count, even, odd

Responding Answers:
Draw Children find page 5 and draw 21 shoes.
Tell About Children tell that there are 21 shoes. They tell that there is one shoe without the matching shoe.
Write Children write: *21 in all*

Strawberries
by Taneesha Campbell illustrated by John Kurtz

Focus: place value through 99

Story Summary: In *Strawberries*, foxes Tina and Theo set out to pick strawberries for Grandpa. They fill 9 buckets with 10 berries in each bucket. Grandpa uses them to make lots of strawberry cakes, and all the foxes from around come to the party.

Vocabulary: tens, place value

Responding Answers:
Draw Children find page 5 and draw 4 buckets.
Tell About Children tell that the foxes have picked 8 buckets and have 80 strawberries.
Write Children write: *80 in all.*

Juggling
by Flora Sanchez illustrated by Barry Gott

Focus: addition and subtraction facts through 12

Story Summary: In *Juggling*, Jerry wants to juggle 12 balls. As soon as he gets them in the air, five drop. His friend Cara throws him two more, but Jerry drops one. Cara throws the last ball, Jerry gets them all in the air, and they all fall down on the laughing children.

Vocabulary: how many, add, subtract

Responding Answers:
Draw Children find page 3 and draw 7 red balls and 5 blue balls.
Tell About Children tell that Jerry dropped 5 balls and is still juggling 7 balls.
Write Children write: *12 balls in all*

Throw That Ball!
by Jay Hanna Dean illustrated by Keiko Motoyama

Focus: graphing and probability

Story Summary: In *Throw That Ball!*, Teddy and Hector try to win prizes at the carnival game in which they throw a ball to knock milk cans down. The prizes are on shelves and there are different numbers of each. Readers are asked which toy the boys will least likely or most likely win.

Vocabulary: more likely, less likely, certain, impossible

Responding Answers:
Draw Children find page 3 and draw 3 shelves with 1 green truck on the bottom, 3 orange trucks on the middle, and 5 blue trucks on the top.
Tell About Children tell that Teddy is more likely to win the a blue truck because there are more of them.
Write Children write: *the green truck.*

Time to Play
by Suki Sataka illustrated by Ana Ochoa

Focus: time

Story Summary: In *Time to Play*, Mark and Mary are going to eat lunch at 12:00. A clock shows 11:00, and Mark and Mary feed their pets until lunch time. At 11:30, Mary reads an analog clock, and Mark reads a digital clock. Finally, it is time to eat.

Vocabulary: time, hour, half-hour, o'clock

Responding Answers:
Draw Children find pages 4 and 5 and draw an analog and a digital clock, both showing 11:30.
Tell About Children tell that both clocks show 11:30, and one is an analog clock and the other is a digital clock.
Write Children write: *both clocks show 11:30.*

What Next?
by Luz Vega illustrated by Gina Fresehet

Focus: patterns

Story Summary: In *What Next?*, Bob the bulldog is a builder. For everything he does, he works in a pattern: painting walls; building houses; cutting out shapes; hours working each day; building birdhouses; wearing T-shirts.

Vocabulary: pattern, color, shape, size

Responding Answers:
Draw Children find page 6 and draw the first 3 houses: small, medium, and large.
Tell About Children tell that the next 3 birdhouses will be small, medium, and large.
Write Children write: *small, medium, and large.*

Pick a Number!

Draw a Picture

Pick a number from 6 to 10.

Draw and color that many flowers.

Write the number of flowers you drew.

Try This

Write the name of the number of flowers you drew.

_____

_____

Sure Shapes

Draw a Picture

Pick a number from 1 to 5.

Draw and color that number of squares.

Write the number of squares you drew.

Try This

Write the name of the number of squares you drew.

_____

_____

Cool Comparisons

Draw a Picture

Draw another set of bugs that *is greater than* this set.

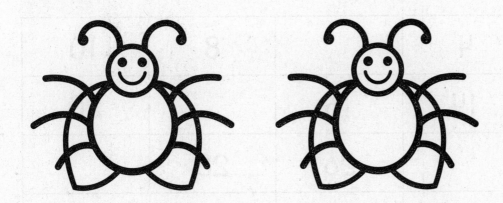

Try This

Write the name of the number of bugs you drew.

_____

_____

Skip It

Write Numbers

Look at the chart. Fill in the missing numbers.

2	4		8	10
	14	16		20
22		26	28	
32			38	

Try This

Pick one of the missing numbers.

Write its name.

_____

_____

Five Alive!

Write Numbers

Look at the chart. Fill in the numbers that are missing.

5	10		20	
30		40	45	50
	60		70	
80		90		100

Try This

Pick one of the missing numbers.

Write its name.

_____

_____

Double Digit

Write Numbers

Look at the chart. Fill in the numbers that are missing.

100	20		80	
	50			
20				*

Try This

Pick one of the missing numbers.

Write its name.

_____

_____

Sum Sentences

Draw a Picture

Color the picture.
Use **2** colors.

Write an addition sentence for it.

Try This

How many balloons are in each part?

Write the number words for each part.

_____

_____

_____

Name _____ Date _____

Put It Together

Draw a Picture

Color these shapes to show **2** parts.

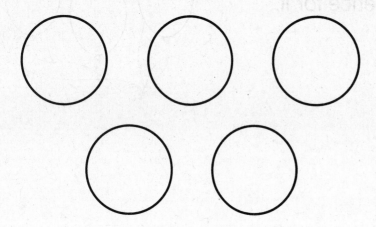

Try This

Are these circles or triangles? Write the name of
the shapes.

_____

_____

How Many Ways?

Draw a Picture

Pick a number from 5 to 10.

How many ways can you show the number?

Draw a picture of the ways.

 Try This

How many ways did you show? Write the number.

_____

_____

20 Through 50

Draw a Picture

Barb has 24 buttons.

Ken has fewer. Ann has more.

Pick Ken or Ann.

Draw the buttons he or she might have.

Try This

A dozen is 12.

How many dozen does Barb have?

Write the number.

_____

_____

Name _____ Date _____

More or Less

Draw a Picture

Look at this picture. Now draw 10 more triangles.
Is 21 less than or more than the number of triangles?

Try This

How many is 10 more than the number of shapes
you see now?

Write the name of the number.

_____

_____

Put Them in Order

Write Numbers

Pick 3 numbers from 1 to 99. Write them from least to greatest. Pick 3 new numbers from 1 to 99. Write them from greatest to least.

least ————————→ greatest

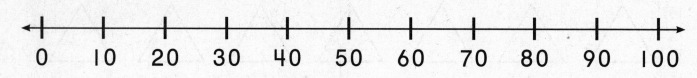

least ←———————— greatest

Try This

Write the name of one number you picked.

_____

_____

Name _____ Date _____

Apples Away

Draw a Picture

Draw 4 apples.

Pick a number from 1 to 3.

Draw legs on that many apples.

Try This

Write a subtraction sentence to tell about your picture.

_____

_____

Runaway Squares

Draw a Picture

Draw 5 squares.

Pick a number from 1 to 4.

Draw legs on that many squares.

Try This

Write a subtraction sentence that tells about your picture.

_____

_____

Plus and Minus

Draw a Picture

Draw **9** oranges.

Pick a number from **3** to **8**. Put legs on that many oranges.

Try This

Write a subtraction sentence for your picture.

_____

_____

_____

Tally Ho!

Make a Chart

Make a tally chart. Color the leaves. Show 5 red leaves. Show 7 yellow leaves.

red	
yellow	

Try This

Are there more red leaves or more yellow leaves?

Write your answer.

_____

_____

Graph Math

Make a Graph

Make a graph of these shapes. □ ○ □ ○ □ ○ □

○	
□	

Try This

Are there more circles or more squares?

Write the name of the number of squares.

_____

_____

Picture Perfect

Make a Chart

Finish this chart. Count the children in your class.
Draw a dot for each boy or girl.

My Class	
boy	
girl	

Try This

Write how many girls there are.

_____

_____

Double Trouble

Draw a Picture

Draw Ted's 5 hats and Ken's 5 hats.

How many hats do they have in all?

Write a number sentence to solve.

 **Try This**

Write the word name for 10.

_____

_____

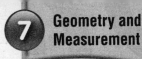

Name _____ Date _____

Back and Forth

Draw a Picture

Draw 2 rows of 10 circles.

Use two colors to show these number sentences:

$2 + 8 = 10$ $8 + 2 = 10$

Try This

Write the two colors you used.

_____

_____

Another Way to Add

Use a Number Line

Use 3 colors to show this number sentence on a number line.

$4 + 3 =$ _____

Circle the sum on the number line.

Fill in the sum in the number sentence.

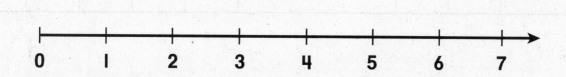

0   1   2   3   4   5   6   7

Try This

Write the word name of the sum.

_____

_____

Spin Around

Use a Chart

Toss a coin.

Will it land more times on *heads* or *tails*? Toss it 10 times. Show the results on a chart.

heads									
tails									

Try This

How many times did the coin land on *heads*?

Write the name of the number.

_____

_____

Pass the Bar

Use a Graph

Make a bar graph. Use these shapes.

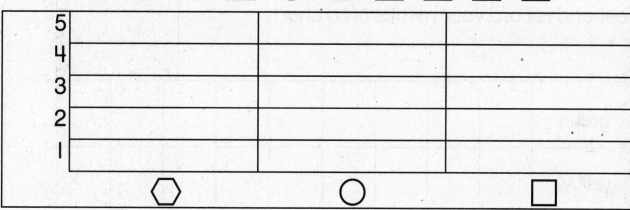

Try This

How many squares are there?

Write the name of the number.

_____

_____

How Likely Is It?

Use a Chart

Draw 10 fish on some paper. Color some green and some yellow. Cut them out and put them in a bag. Which color are you more likely to pick? Why? Test and record your results on a chart.

green										
yellow										

Try This

Write the name of the color you picked most.

_____

_____

Subtract!

Draw a Picture

Color these 5 dragonflies.

Color some of them green and some of them red.

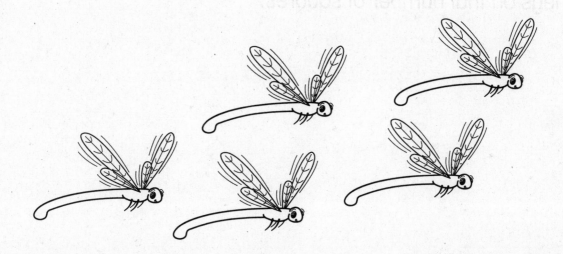

Try This

Are there more or fewer red dragonflies?

Write your answer.

_____

_____

Picture This

Draw a Picture

Draw 6 squares. Color them.

Pick a number from 1 to 5.

Draw legs on that number of squares.

How many are left? Write the name of the number.

_____

_____

Close Relatives

Draw a Picture

Color **2** rows of **5** squares. Show each number sentence.

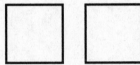 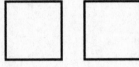 

$2 + 3 = 5$

$5 - 2 = 3$

Try This

What colors did you use?

Write the names.

_____

_____

More Alike Than Not

Draw a Picture

Draw **3** shapes with **3** sides.

Do not make them exactly the same.

How many corners does each have?

Try This

Write the name of the shape you drew.

_____

_____

On the Corner

Draw a Picture

Draw shapes that have **4** corners.

Try This

Write how many sides your shapes have.

_____

_____

Building Blocks

Draw a Picture

Draw a car. Use these shapes.

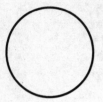  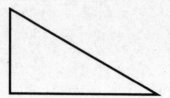

Try This

How many circles did you use?

Write the name of the number.

_____

_____

Face Facts

Draw a Picture

Draw 12 suns.

Circle some.

Write a fact family.

 **Try This**

How many suns did you circle?

Write the number name.

_____

_____

Any Way You Cut It

Draw a Picture

Pick a number from 1 to 12.

Draw 2 ways of showing that number.

 Try This

Write the name of the number you chose.

_____

_____

Problem Solving

Draw a Picture

Ann has 5 cars.

Ben has 6 cars.

How many cars do they have? Draw the cars.

Try This

How many cars do they have?

Write the number name.

_____

_____

Number Patterns

Write Numbers

Color the numbers in this pattern.

Write the number that comes next.

3 5 3 5

Try This

Did you write three or five? Write the name of the number you wrote.

_____

_____

Shapes Alive

Draw a Picture

Color the pattern. Draw what comes next.

Try This

Are these squares, circles, or triangles?

Write the name of the first shape in the pattern.

_____

_____

True Colors

Draw a Picture

Color this pattern. Use **2** colors.

Draw and color what comes next.

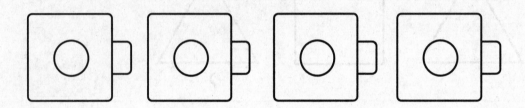

Try This

Did you use green, red, or blue? Write the name of
a color you used.

_____

_____

Name _____ Date _____

Capacity

Draw a Picture

Draw these bowls in size order.

The first bowl should hold the most.

The last bowl should hold the least.

Try This

Which bowl can hold the biggest number of cubes?

Write your answer.

_____

_____

Name _____ Date _____

Heavy and Light

Make a Chart

Fill in the chart.

Write the word *light* or *heavy* next to each item.

chair	
desk	
chalk	
pencil	

Try This

Which item do you think is the heaviest?

Write your answer.

_____

_____

Hot and Cold

Draw a Picture

Draw your favorite dinner.

Label foods *hot* or *cold*.

Try This

Do you like hot food or cold food best?

Why? Write your answer.

_____

_____

Name _____ Date _____

Teen Time

Use a Chart

Show the number 12 on the chart with beads, buttons, or bows.

Tens	Ones

Try This

Write the name of what you drew.

_____

_____

Groups of Ten

Draw a Picture

Draw 10 squares.

Draw a circle around the group.

Then draw 10 more squares.

Circle that group.

(Try This)

How many squares did you draw in all?

Write the number.

_____

_____

Ten and Up

Draw a Picture

12 eggs make a dozen.

Draw 2 dozen brown eggs.

Circle 2 groups of 10 eggs.

How many eggs are there in all?

Write the number.

Try This

Write the name of the number.

_____

_____

A Nickel Is Five

Draw a Picture

Ira has 3 nickels.

Pam has 3 pennies.

Who has the coins of greater value?

Draw a picture to solve.

Try This

How many cents does Pam have?

Write the number name.

_____

_____

Name _____ Date _____

A Pretty Penny

Draw a Picture

Bob has 4¢.

Dan has 3¢.

How many pennies do they have?

Draw a picture to solve.

Try This

How many more pennies does Bob have? Write the
number name.

_____

_____

Dime Store

Draw a Picture

Kit has 4 dimes and Mel has 5 dimes.

A toy costs 80¢.

Can they buy it?

Draw a picture of their coins to solve.

Try This

Do they have more or less money than they need?

Write your answer.

_____

_____

_____

Make a Ten to Add

Draw a Picture

There are 8 sheep in the barn. 6 sheep come in to sleep. How many sheep are there in all? Draw a picture to solve. Draw Xs for the sheep.

Try This

Finish: 8 sheep plus 2 sheep is _____ sheep.

Write the missing number name.

_____

_____

Add With Ten

Draw a Picture

Liz has 10 eggs. She puts 8 more in the basket. How many eggs does she have now? Draw a picture to solve.

Try This

How many eggs are there in all?

Write the number.

_____

_____

The Sum Is the Same

Draw a Picture

Sue has 13 seeds. Al and Ed want some. How can
Sue divide the seeds? Draw a picture to solve.

Try This

If Sue gives 4 to Al, how many will Ed get?

Write your answer.

_____

_____

Name _____ Date _____

Half Past

Draw a Picture

Kit walked her dog. She left at 5 o'clock and returned at 5:30. How long was she gone? Draw the times to solve.

Try This

How long is a half-hour?

Write your answer.

_____

_____

_____

On the Hour

Draw a Picture

Ted goes to bed at **8:00**. Alma goes to bed at **9:00**. Draw the times to show when they go to bed.

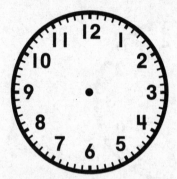 

Try This

What time do you go to bed?

Write the hour.

_____

_____

Time Passes

Draw a Picture

Ken is up at **7:30** and is at camp at **9:00**.
How long does it take him to get to camp? Draw the
times to solve.

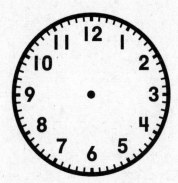 

Try This

Ken gets home at **4:30**.

How long is he at camp?

Write your answer.

_____

_____

_____

Interchange

Draw a Picture

Draw 12 shells. Circle some. Write 2 subtraction sentences about your picture.

(Try This)

How many shells did you circle?

Write the name of the number.

_____

_____

The Missing Piece

Draw a Picture

Look at the picture. It shows 1 addend in the addition sentence $7 + \square = 10$. Draw the missing addend.

Try This

Write the name of the shapes you drew.

_____

_____

Number Tales

Draw a Picture

Look at the picture. Color the beach towels.
Circle some of them. Write a number sentence
about them.

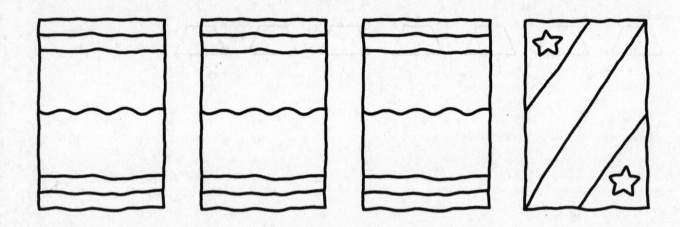

Try This

Write about the picture.

_____

_____

_____

Parting Company

Draw a Picture

Color a pizza. Add all your favorite toppings. Then mark the pizza with **2** lines to show **4** equal parts.

Try This

What number rhymes with the word *more*?

Write the number name.

_____

_____

Half Math

Draw a Picture

Fold a piece of paper in half.

Draw this picture. Hold the fold.
Cut on the line you drew.

Open it up!

Try This

Write the number of equal parts you made.

_____

_____

Partners

Draw a Picture

Draw **8** circles.

Color some red and the rest purple.

Write about your picture. Use the words *out of*.

_____

_____

Regroup

Draw a Picture

Liz has 17 pennies.

Bob has 9 pennies.

How many do they have in all?

Draw the pennies in groups of 10.

Try This

Write a number sentence to solve.

_____

_____

Count On

Draw a Picture

Fran has 14 red beads.

Ned has 3 blue beads.

How many do they have in all?

Draw to solve.

Try This

Write an addition sentence for your picture. _____

_____

_____

Neat Trick

Draw a Picture

Bill had **27** guppies.

He got **8** more.

How many does he have in all?

Draw a dot for each guppy.

Write an addition sentence to solve.

Try This

Bill's tank can hold **40** guppies. Write how many more will fit.

_____

_____

_____

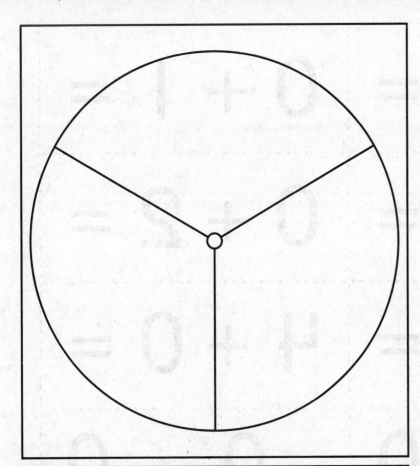

Spinner Tips

How to assemble spinner.
- Glue patterns to tagboard.
- Cut out and attach pointer with a fastener.

Alternative
- Children can use a paper clip and pencil instead.

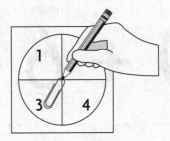

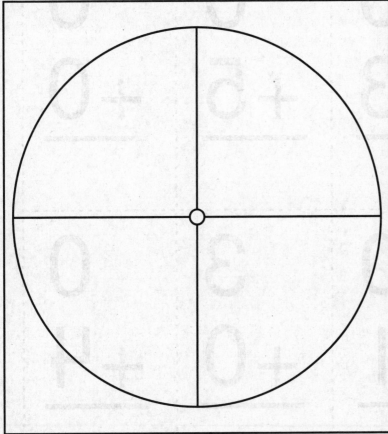

© Houghton Mifflin Harcourt Publishing Company

$$5 + 0 =$$

$$0 + 1 =$$

$$3 + 0 =$$

$$0 + 2 =$$

$$0 + 6 =$$

$$4 + 0 =$$

$$\begin{array}{r} 6 \\ +0 \\ \hline \end{array}$$

$$\begin{array}{r} 0 \\ +3 \\ \hline \end{array}$$

$$\begin{array}{r} 0 \\ +5 \\ \hline \end{array}$$

$$\begin{array}{r} 0 \\ +0 \\ \hline \end{array}$$

$$\begin{array}{r} 2 \\ +0 \\ \hline \end{array}$$

$$\begin{array}{r} 0 \\ +1 \\ \hline \end{array}$$

$$\begin{array}{r} 3 \\ +0 \\ \hline \end{array}$$

$$\begin{array}{r} 0 \\ +4 \\ \hline \end{array}$$

$$4 + 1 =$$

$$1 + 4 =$$

$$3 + 2 =$$

$$2 + 3 =$$

$$3 + 0 =$$

$$0 + 3 =$$

$$\begin{array}{r} 2 \\ +1 \\ \hline \end{array}$$

$$\begin{array}{r} 1 \\ +2 \\ \hline \end{array}$$

$$\begin{array}{r} 3 \\ +2 \\ \hline \end{array}$$

$$\begin{array}{r} 2 \\ +3 \\ \hline \end{array}$$

$$\begin{array}{r} 5 \\ +3 \\ \hline \end{array}$$

$$\begin{array}{r} 3 \\ +5 \\ \hline \end{array}$$

$$\begin{array}{r} 6 \\ +4 \\ \hline \end{array}$$

$$\begin{array}{r} 4 \\ +6 \\ \hline \end{array}$$

7 + 1 =   8 + 0 =

6 + 2 =   4 + 4 =

5 + 3 =   2 + 6 =

$$\begin{array}{r} 3 \\ +5 \\ \hline \end{array}$$
$$\begin{array}{r} 1 \\ +7 \\ \hline \end{array}$$
$$\begin{array}{r} 4 \\ +4 \\ \hline \end{array}$$
$$\begin{array}{r} 2 \\ +6 \\ \hline \end{array}$$

$$\begin{array}{r} 7 \\ +1 \\ \hline \end{array}$$
$$\begin{array}{r} 0 \\ +8 \\ \hline \end{array}$$
$$\begin{array}{r} 5 \\ +3 \\ \hline \end{array}$$
$$\begin{array}{r} 8 \\ +0 \\ \hline \end{array}$$

$$5 + 3 =$$

$$4 + 8 =$$

$$2 + 5 =$$

$$6 + 1 =$$

$$7 + 2 =$$

$$5 + 4 =$$

$$\begin{array}{r} 4 \\ +2 \\ \hline \end{array}$$

$$\begin{array}{r} 7 \\ +3 \\ \hline \end{array}$$

$$\begin{array}{r} 1 \\ +2 \\ \hline \end{array}$$

$$\begin{array}{r} 3 \\ +6 \\ \hline \end{array}$$

$$\begin{array}{r} 8 \\ +0 \\ \hline \end{array}$$

$$\begin{array}{r} 3 \\ +2 \\ \hline \end{array}$$

$$\begin{array}{r} 4 \\ +5 \\ \hline \end{array}$$

$$\begin{array}{r} 6 \\ +2 \\ \hline \end{array}$$

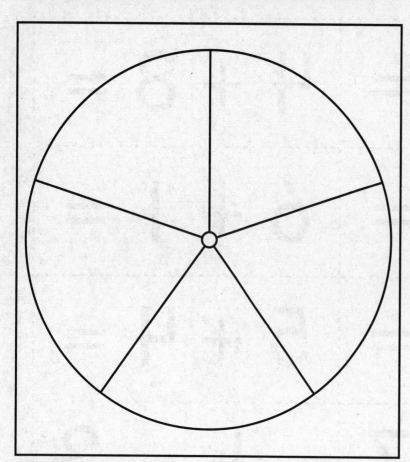

Spinner Tips

How to assemble spinner.
- Glue patterns to tagboard.
- Cut out and attach pointer with a fastener.

Alternative
- Children can use a paper clip and pencil instead.

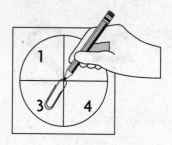

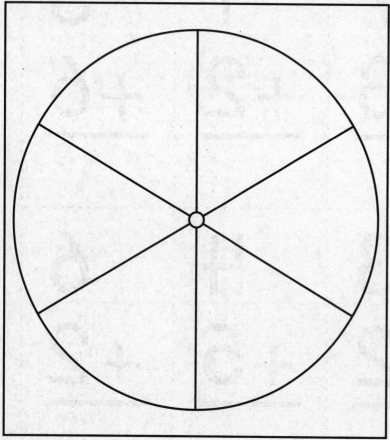

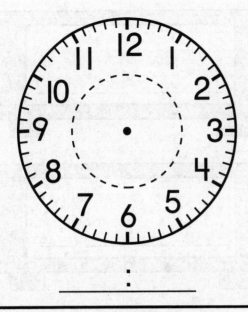

_____ : _____

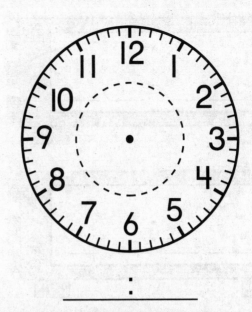

_____ : _____

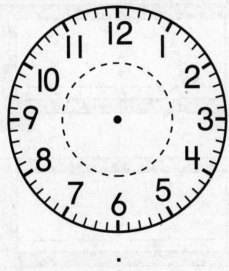

_____ : _____

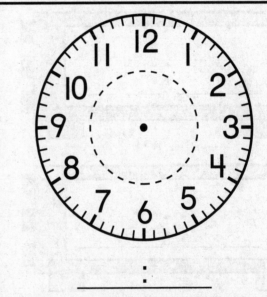

_____ : _____

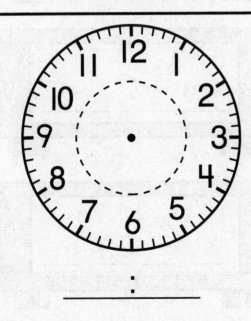

_____ : _____

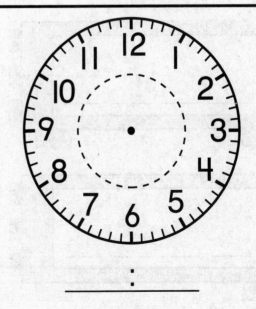

_____ : _____

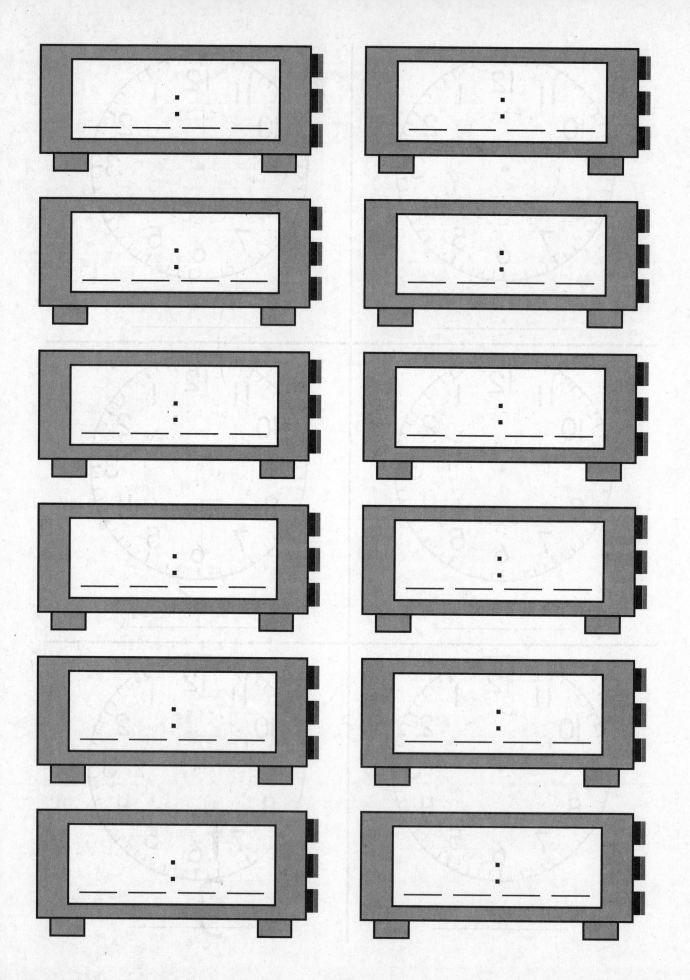

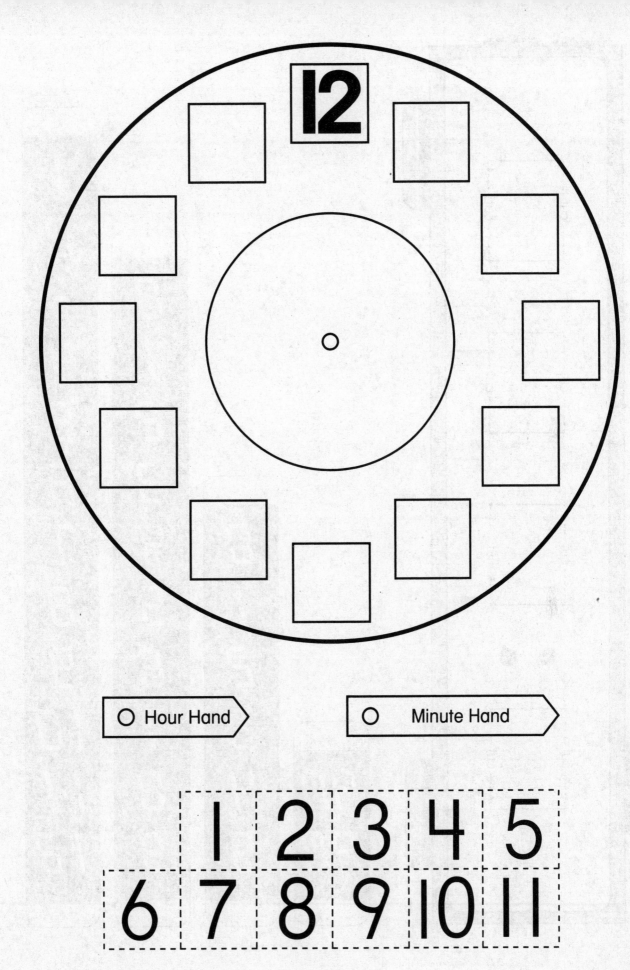

Minute Hand

1 2 3 4 5
6 7 8 9 10 11

Grab-and-Go!™ Teacher Guide and Activity Resources   **105**   **Analog Clock Model**
© Houghton Mifflin Harcourt Publishing Company

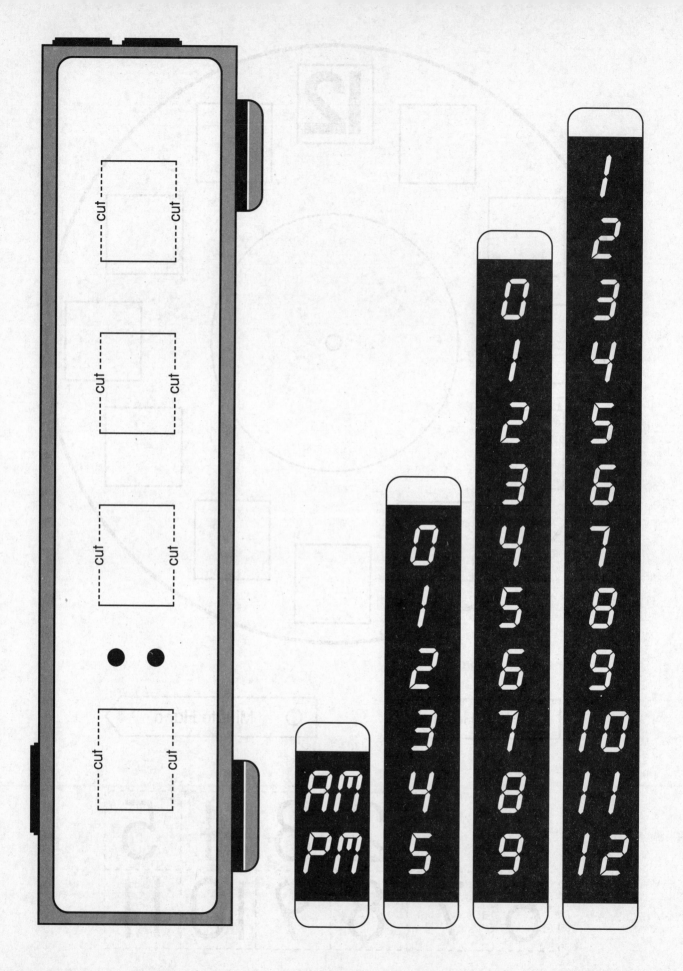

6 – 0 =   6 – 6 =

3 – 0 =   4 – 4 =

3 – 3 =   4 – 0 =

$$\begin{array}{r} 2 \\ -2 \\ \hline \end{array}$$
$$\begin{array}{r} 5 \\ -5 \\ \hline \end{array}$$
$$\begin{array}{r} 2 \\ -0 \\ \hline \end{array}$$
$$\begin{array}{r} 5 \\ -0 \\ \hline \end{array}$$

$$\begin{array}{r} 1 \\ -0 \\ \hline \end{array}$$
$$\begin{array}{r} 1 \\ -1 \\ \hline \end{array}$$
$$\begin{array}{r} 0 \\ -0 \\ \hline \end{array}$$
$$\begin{array}{r} 6 \\ -6 \\ \hline \end{array}$$

5 − 3 =   8 − 4 =

6 − 5 =   4 − 2 =

7 − 1 =   5 − 2 =

$$\begin{array}{r} 8 \\ -5 \\ \hline \end{array}$$ $$\begin{array}{r} 6 \\ -3 \\ \hline \end{array}$$ $$\begin{array}{r} 7 \\ -4 \\ \hline \end{array}$$ $$\begin{array}{r} 3 \\ -1 \\ \hline \end{array}$$

$$\begin{array}{r} 2 \\ -1 \\ \hline \end{array}$$ $$\begin{array}{r} 8 \\ -3 \\ \hline \end{array}$$ $$\begin{array}{r} 4 \\ -2 \\ \hline \end{array}$$ $$\begin{array}{r} 3 \\ -2 \\ \hline \end{array}$$

7 − 2 =   9 − 0 =

10 − 6 =   6 − 2 =

5 − 4 =   7 − 3 =

```
  6        9        1        6
− 1      − 4      − 0      − 4
———      ———      ———      ———
```

```
  7        5        8        3
− 5      − 2      − 3      − 1
———      ———      ———      ———
```

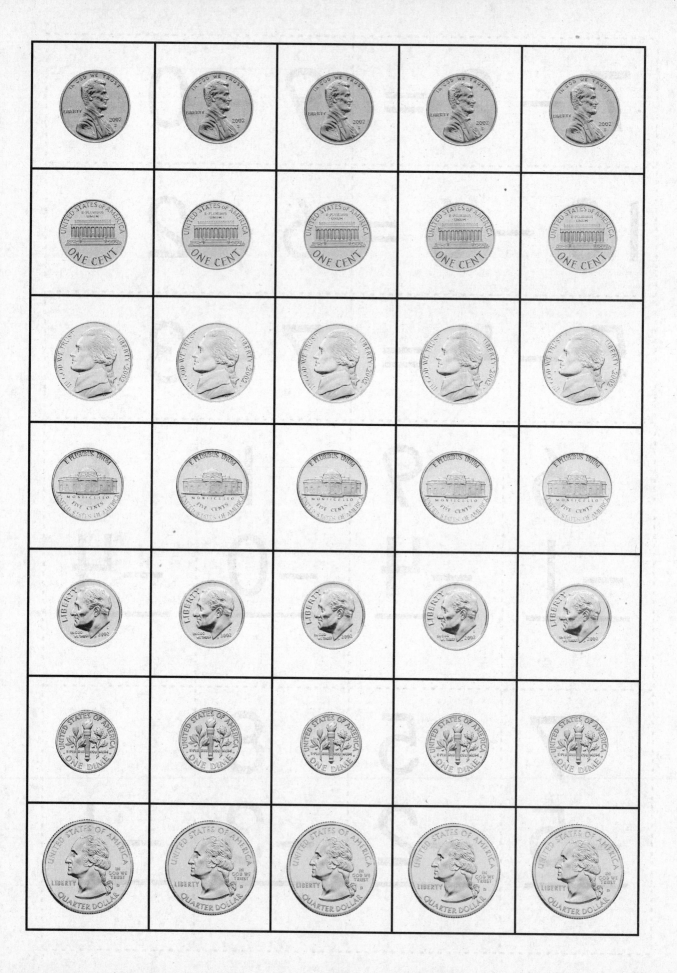

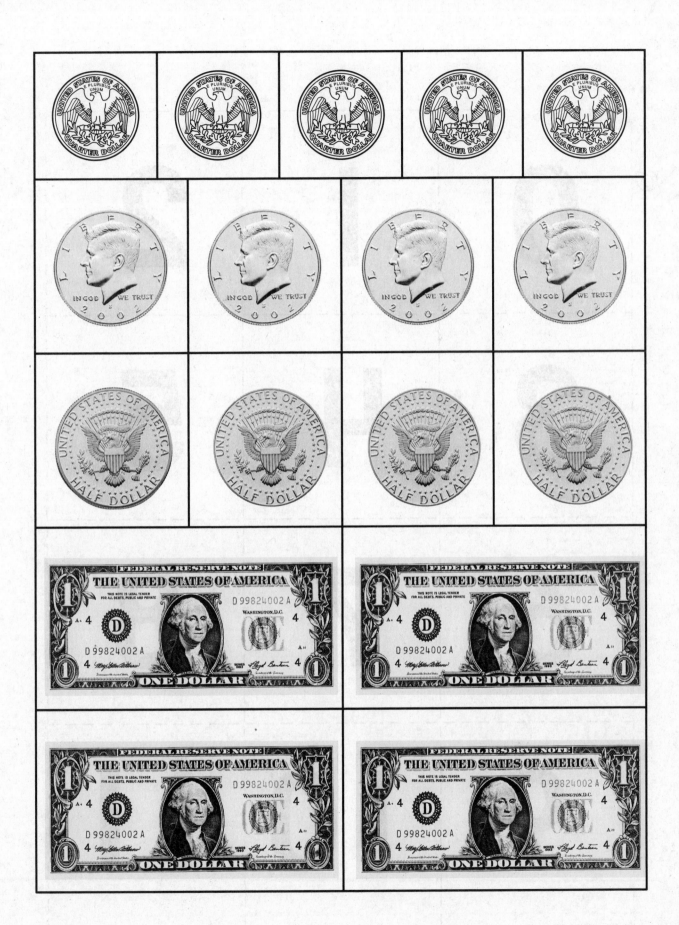

0	1	2
3	4	5
6	7	8
9	10	11

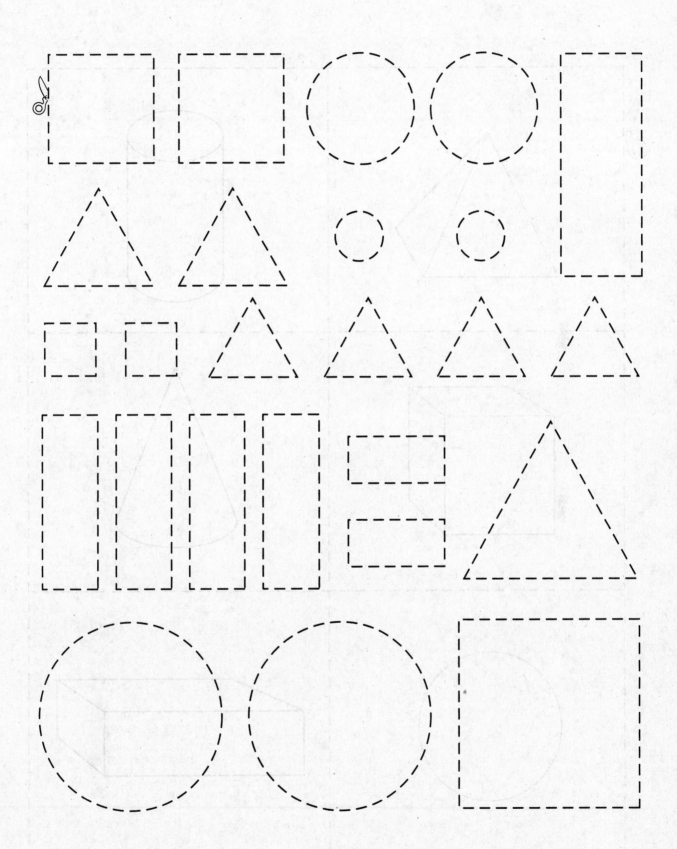

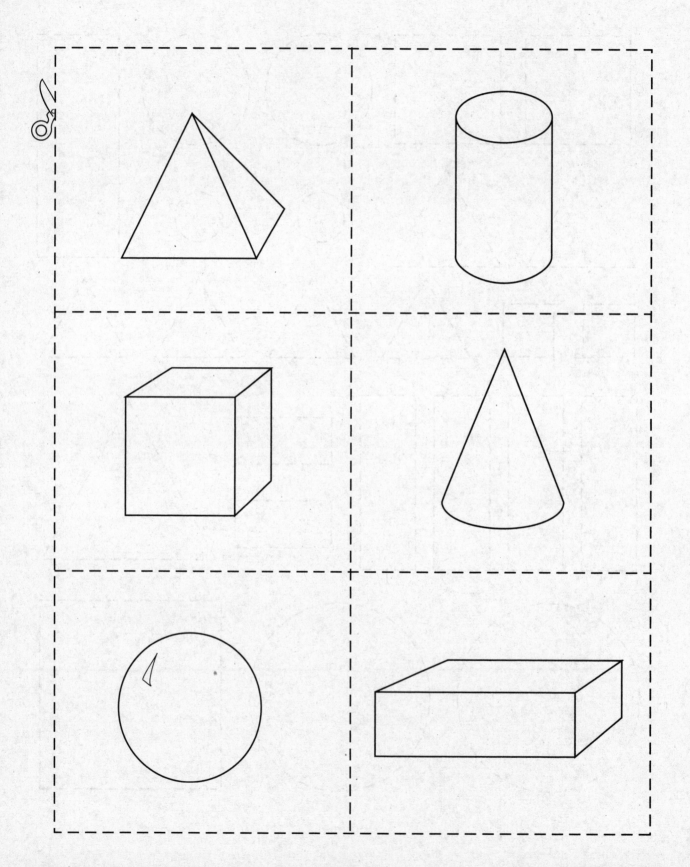

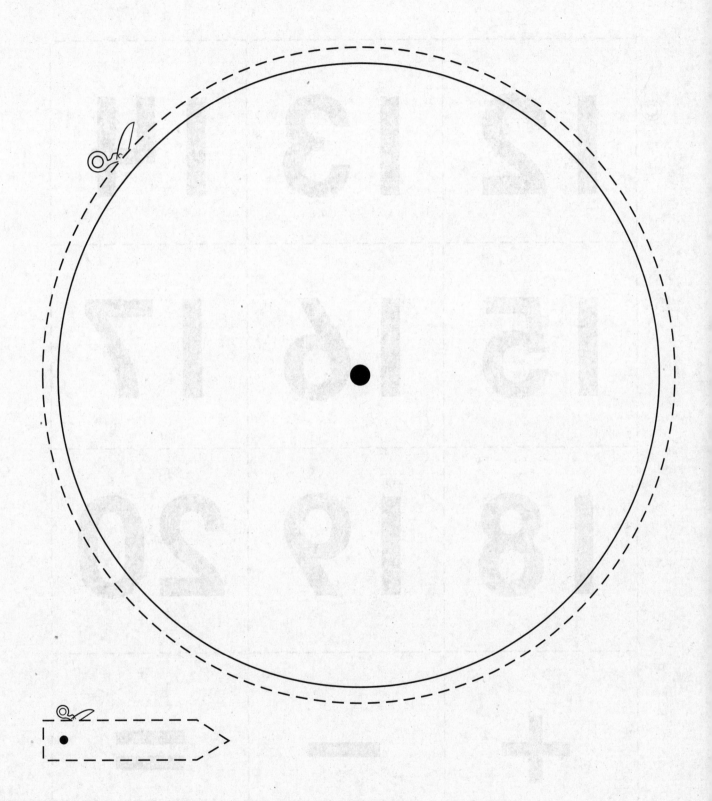

12	13	14
15	16	17
18	19	20
+	−	=

Workmat 1 Multi-Purpose Mat

Workmat 2 Part-Part-Whole Model

Whole

Part

Part

Workmat 3
Tens and Ones Chart

Tens	Ones

Workmat 4
Hundred Chart

1	2	3	4	5	6	7	8	9	10
11	12	13	14	15	16	17	18	19	20
21	22	23	24	25	26	27	28	29	30
31	32	33	34	35	36	37	38	39	40
41	42	43	44	45	46	47	48	49	50
51	52	53	54	55	56	57	58	59	60
61	62	63	64	65	66	67	68	69	70
71	72	73	74	75	76	77	78	79	80
81	82	83	84	85	86	87	88	89	90
91	92	93	94	95	96	97	98	99	100

Workmat 5 Ten Frame

Workmat 6 Ten Frames

Workmat 7 Number Lines 1–60

20 19 18 17 16 15 14 13 12 11 10 9 8 7 6 5 4 3 2 1

40 39 38 37 36 35 34 33 32 31 30 29 28 27 26 25 24 23 22 21

60 59 58 57 56 55 54 53 52 51 50 49 48 47 46 45 44 43 42 41